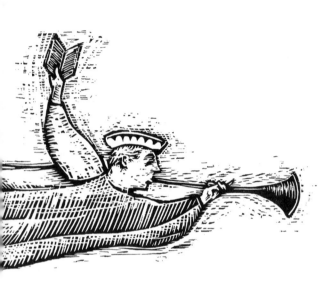

Enos, Jarom, Omni: *a brief theological introduction*

This publication was made possible by generous support from the Laura F. Willes Center for Book of Mormon Studies, part of the Neal A. Maxwell Institute for Religious Scholarship at Brigham Young University.

Published by the Neal A. Maxwell Institute for Religious Scholarship, Brigham Young University, Provo, Utah. The copyright for the 2013 text of The Book of Mormon is held by The Church of Jesus Christ of Latter-day Saints, Salt Lake City, Utah; that text is quoted throughout and used by permission.

The Maxwell Institute's *The Book of Mormon: brief theological introductions* series is not made, provided, approved, or endorsed by Intellectual Reserve Inc. or The Church of Jesus Christ of Latter-day Saints. Any content or opinions expressed, implied, or included in or with this book are solely those of the author and are not necessarily those of Brigham Young University or any of its affiliates, Intellectual Reserve, Inc., or The Church of Jesus Christ of Latter-day Saints.

Printed in the United States of America

ISBN: 978-0-8425-0015-9
LIBRARY OF CONGRESS CONTROL NUMBER: 2020902481

Enos, Jarom, Omni

a brief theological introduction

BRIGHAM YOUNG UNIVERSITY

NEAL A. MAXWELL INSTITUTE

PROVO, UTAH

Sharon J. Harris

The Book of Mormon: brief theological introductions series seeks Christ in scripture by combining intellectual rigor and the disciple's yearning for holiness. It answers Elder Neal A. Maxwell's call to explore the book's "divine architecture": "There is so much more in the Book of Mormon than we have yet discovered. The book's divine architecture and rich furnishings will increasingly unfold to our view, further qualifying it as *'a marvelous work and a wonder.'* (Isaiah 29:14) . . . All the rooms in this mansion need to be explored, whether by valued traditional scholars or by those at the cutting edge. Each plays a role, and one LDS scholar cannot say to the other, *'I have no need of thee.'"* [1] (1 Corinthians 12:21)

For some time, faithful scholars have explored the book's textual history, reception, historicity, literary quality, and more. This series focuses particularly on theology—the scholarly practice of exploring a scriptural text's implications and its lens on God's work in the world. Series volumes invite Latter-day Saints to discover additional dimensions of this treasured text but leave to prophets and apostles their unique role of declaring its definitive official doctrines. In this case, theology, as opposed to authoritative doctrine, relates to the original sense of the term as, literally, reasoned "God talk." The word also designates a well-developed academic field, but it is the more general sense of the term that most often applies here. By engaging each scriptural book's theology on its own terms, this series explores the spiritual and intellectual force of the ideas appearing in the Latter-day Saints' "keystone" scripture.

Series authors and editors possess specialized professional training that informs their work but, significantly, each takes Christ as theology's proper end because he is the proper end of all scripture and all reflection on it. We, too, "talk of Christ, we rejoice in Christ, we preach of Christ...that our children may know to what source they may look for a remission of their sins" (2 Nephi 25:26). Moreover, while experts in the modern disciplines of philosophy, theology, literature, and history, series authors and editors also work explicitly within the context of personal and institutional commitments both to Christian discipleship and to The Church of Jesus Christ of Latter-day Saints. These volumes are not official Church publications but can be best understood in light of these deep commitments. And because we acknowledge that scripture demands far more than intellectual experimentation, we call readers' attention to the processes of conversion and sanctification at play on virtually every scriptural page.

Individual series authors offer unique approaches but, taken together, they model a joint invitation to readers to engage scripture in their own way. No single approach to theology or scriptural interpretation commands preeminence in these volumes. No volume pretends to be the final word on theological reflection for its part of the Book of Mormon. Varied perspectives and methodologies are evident throughout. This is intentional. In addition, though we recognize love for the Book of Mormon is a "given" for most Latter-day Saint readers, we also share the conviction that, like the gospel of Jesus Christ itself, the Book of Mormon is inexhaustible.[2] These volumes invite readers to slow down and read scripture more thoughtfully and transformatively. Elder Maxwell cautioned against reading the Book of Mormon as "hurried tourists" who scarcely venture beyond "the entry hall."[3] To that end, we dedicate this series to his apostolic conviction that there is always more to learn from the Book of Mormon and much to be gained from our faithful search for Christ in its pages.

—The Editors

Contents

Introduction

Chances are decent that you're holding and reading this book right now as a kind of dare. In a series of short theological introductions, perhaps it seems obvious why. First, Second, and Third Nephi merit standalone volumes. But Enos, Jarom, and Omni? These are the flyover books. Upon hearing of Jesus, Nathanael's first reaction was, "Can there any good thing come out of Nazareth?"(John 1:46). Likewise, in our first reaction to Enos, Jarom, and Omni we might wonder, can any theology come out of these itty bitty books, as I have affectionately come to call them? Read and see.[1]

Let's get our bearings. The books of Enos, Jarom, and Omni cover a lot of ground in a few pages. They comprise the end of the small plates, a volume Nephi forged as a record separate from the large plates that contain the political history of his people. For this reason, they're our last taste of the non-abridged portion of the Book of Mormon. After them, we move on to Mormon and Moroni's abridgments and compilations. Enos, Jarom, and Omni span nearly four hundred years (roughly 500–150 BC) and introduce us to numerous peoples beyond the Nephite and Lamanite nations: the Mulekites, the Jaredites, and the followers of Zeniff. We encounter seven different writers in these books, the eponymous authors of Enos and Jarom, and five contributors to the book of Omni. Seven writers across almost four centuries and at least five different political peoples, all in only seventy-two verses. (By contrast, a single chapter in Jacob runs to seventy-seven verses.) Such compact treatment makes for a

30,000-foot view not often glimpsed elsewhere in the Book of Mormon. What can we see from such a height? Zooming out in these books reveals two themes: covenant and inheritance.

the covenant of the Book of Mormon

First, the theme of covenant takes center stage. This is the engine that propels the Book of Mormon as a whole and the small plates in particular, and nowhere is the covenant outlined more clearly than in Enos. With talk of the covenant, we don't mean individual covenants each of us makes with God, like, baptism, for example. We mean something bigger, with repercussions in Enos continuing into the books of Jarom and Omni. What is this Book of Mormon covenant? We find various statements of it from Lehi, Nephi, and Jacob—and then especially from Jesus Christ later in the volume. For our purposes, though, Enos summarizes it best:

> If it should so be, that my people, the Nephites, should fall into transgression, and by any means be destroyed, and the Lamanites should not be destroyed, that the Lord God would preserve a record of my people, the Nephites . . . that it might be brought forth at some future day unto the Lamanites, that, perhaps, they might be brought unto salvation. . . . I did cry unto God that he would preserve the records; and he covenanted with me that he would bring them forth unto the Lamanites in his own due time (Enos 1:13, 16).

In short, the covenant is God's promise to gather the descendants of Lehi and Sariah's family again. God will do so by making sure that the surviving remnant of this line of the house of Israel receives the record of their ancestors, the Book of Mormon. When the covenant appears in the text, God also stresses that the gathering will happen on this land to which the first family came. This "holy land," as God tells Enos, is the setting for these covenants and prophecies to be fulfilled (Enos 1:10).

The Book of Mormon's title page says this covenant is the purpose of the book. And it lists Israel's remnant as its first intended recipients: "Written to the Lamanites, who are a remnant of the house of Israel," and, farther down, "to show unto the remnant of the house of Israel what great things the Lord hath done for their fathers, and that they may know the covenants of the Lord, that they are not cast off forever" (title page). To fulfill this covenant, then, two things must happen. First, a Lamanite remnant of Lehi and Sariah's family must survive on this land. Second, the record of the Nephite prophets must also survive until it reaches its intended audience in the latter days. Once we recognize this covenant, we see it everywhere in these small books.

inheritance

One way that the burden and awareness of the covenant come up in these books is through the second large-scale theme: inheritance. The plates are an inheritance that travels through time from author to author, usually from one generation to the next. Most of the writers in these small books talk about the responsibility or commandment they inherited to preserve the record and pass it along when the time comes. In this inheritance, they feel obligated to the covenant, and this obligation is weighty enough to sustain the plates' transfer, even to or through some unlikely contributors. Some of them don't say much, but, honoring their receipt of the plates, they perpetuate the record's progress through time. With seven recordkeepers across just a few printed pages, the idea of inheritance recurs frequently.

But the plates are not the only kind of inheritance depicted in these books. Family resemblances (and telling dissimilarities too) show up in the generational hinges between members of the family. Enos, for instance, writes his account to indicate that he takes after both his father, Jacob, and his uncle, Nephi. Jarom structures his values around the revelations that his father, Enos, received, but, as we will see, he also pointedly leaves behind some of his father's worldview. Omni contrasts himself with his righteous father, Jarom. Of Omni's descendants, some adhere closely to the Nephite religious traditions, and others seem to recognize only their familial obligation to preserve the record. Like many other parts of the Book of Mormon, these books of Enos, Jarom, and Omni underscore that this is scripture about families.

We need to pause for a minute here in the introduction to point out an invisibility so complete that it can be distracting: nowhere do the books of Enos, Jarom, and Omni mention or even allude to women. Thus, whatever these books say about families is, of necessity, incomplete. The omission is tragic. We and the Nephites are poorer for it, and we must do better in our own preaching and writing. This said, for the present task we will keep three ideas foregrounded. First, women were part of the Lehite story, even if they were left out of the version we have. Second (and as we will see later in this book), if we think only of nuclear mother-father-children families when we read about families in the scriptures, then we have underrated the scope of God's designs for his children. Third, God's covenants are extended to all of his children; if we don't see some of God's children in the scriptures, we have either misunderstood the scriptures that we have, or we can look forward to receiving more. Thus, in this book, I am assuming that women are included in the theology, even if they are missing from the text.

Returning to the theme of inheritance, later portions of the Book of Mormon echo with their inheritance of and indebtedness to these small books. For example, when Moroni takes over his father's record, he introduces himself as if in imitation of Jacob, Jarom, and Omni: "Behold I, Moroni, do finish the record of my father, Mormon. Behold, I have but few things to write, which things I have been commanded by my father" (Morm. 8:1). Like these earlier writers, Moroni also emphasizes that he will write just a little because of his father's commandment (Jarom 1:1; Omni 1:1). Moroni also closes his writings like they do theirs. He invites his readers to come unto Christ (see Moro. 10:32) in words reminiscent of Amaleki's at the close of Omni (see Omni 1:26), and he bids them farewell and mentions God's judgment bar, as do Jacob and Nephi in their valedictions (see Jacob 6:13; 7:27; 2 Ne. 33:14–15). It's unsurprising that other writers notice how the authors of the small plates' short books begin and end their accounts. We may not be able to say for sure, but it seems plausible that Moroni turned to the short books as inspiration for his beginnings and endings—the rapid turnover of authors in these books certainly provides many examples.

Mormon, too, seems to have paid attention to the content of the small books and used it for his own preaching. Amaleki teaches that "there is nothing which is good save it comes from the Lord: and that which is evil cometh from the devil" (Omni 1:25). Mormon says something very similar: "For every thing which inviteth to do good, and to persuade to believe in Christ, is sent forth by the power and gift of

Christ.... But whatsoever thing persuadeth men to do evil, and believe not in Christ, and deny him, and serve not God, then ye may know with a perfect knowledge it is of the devil" (Moro. 7:16–17). Regardless of whether Mormon took his sermon directly from Amaleki's writings, we know that he read the small plates, and the language and ideas between these passages is very similar. This is not, however, the strongest indication of Mormon's interest in these small books.

Dictation order

One key detail about Mormon's treatment of the small plates not only argues for their importance to the Book of Mormon overall but also foregrounds the message and position of these short books. There's reason to think that Mormon intended his book to end with the small books of Enos, Jarom, and Omni. The Book of Mormon as we read it today is found in roughly chronological order, with 1 Nephi telling the beginnings of Lehite history and Moroni concluding after the Nephites' total destruction. But there's reason to think that, in the actual collection of plates Joseph Smith translated, the small plates (from 1 Nephi through Omni) were placed at the end rather than at the beginning of the record (see FIGURE 1).

If this is right, Enos, Jarom, and Omni were the last books of the whole project as Mormon presented it to be read. Mormon may have organized the record so that these constituted its final message, the last statement that would eventually go to the remnant of the house of Israel. He explains that he found the small plates and elected to "finish [his] record upon them" (W of M 1:5). This sequence (beginning with Mosiah and ending with Omni) can be called the "dictation order" of the Book of Mormon, since it's the order Joseph Smith followed when he dictated the text from

Dictation Order of the Gold Plates

	BOOK / SECTION	SOURCE
Mormon's abridgment	[lost pages] Mosiah (partial) Alma Helaman 3 Nephi 4 Nephi	Large plates of Nephi *abridged by Mormon*
	Mormon 1–7	
Moroni's contribution	Mormon 8–9	
	Ether	Jaredite plates *translated by Mosiah₂* *and abridged by Moroni*
	Moroni Title page	
	1 Nephi 2 Nephi Jacob Enos Jarom Omni	Small plates of Nephi *unabridged*
	Words of Mormon	

FIGURE 1 This chart reflects the best available scholarship for dictation order. Scholars continue to study and debate possible sequences of the Book of Mormon, including Mormon's intended sequence, Moroni's possible rearrangements, and Joseph Smith's dictation order, each of which may have differed from one another.

 Subscripts differentiate Mosiah son of Benjamin (Mosiah₂) from his grandfather (Mosiah₁). Throughout this book series, subscripts similarly distinguish other Book of Mormon figures who share the same name: Alma, Helaman, Nephi, and so forth.

the plates to his scribes. The prophet first translated what we now know as the lost manuscript, which contained Mormon's abridgment of the large plates from the time of Lehi until King Benjamin. After those pages were lost, God instructed the prophet not to go back and retranslate, but instead to pick up where he left off, in what we know as Mosiah.[2] So Joseph Smith continued with Mosiah, Alma, Helaman, 3 Nephi, 4 Nephi, and Mormon. He then translated Moroni's contributions—Mormon 8–9, Ether, and Moroni—before finally translating the small plates and the Words of Mormon. Dictation order is sometimes also called Mormon's order, Mosiah-First, or Mosiah priority.

How does our understanding change when we consider the Book of Mormon in dictation order? For starters, doing so recasts the arc of the Book of Mormon. In dictation order we begin our reading not with 1 Nephi but with Mosiah. We start with the conversion of an entire nation and then the emergence of a Nephite Christian church. That church's growth and challenges are detailed through the books of Alma and Helaman and culminate in 3 Nephi when an apocalypse destroys lands and cities and prefaces the visit of the Lord. When Jesus Christ arrives and teaches the Lehites, he reestablishes the church, ordains leadership, and clarifies and reorients the church's eternal purpose. In particular, Jesus spends much of his time reading and explaining biblical texts and emphasizing the covenant through Isaiah and other prophecies (see 3 Ne. 20–25). He thus introduces what, for readers beginning with Mosiah, is a wholly new theme. The remainder of Mormon and Moroni's records tells stories of decline and destruction but emphasizes also the survival of the Lamanites and promises that they will be redeemed according to the covenant.

But in dictation order, Moroni's final testimony is not the end of the Book of Mormon. Instead, we are alerted to a record that Mormon found while compiling and abridging: a first-person account of the founding family—and a record that provides "greater views" on the gospel and especially on the Book of Mormon covenant (D&C 10:45). After all this time, having watched the progression from national conversion to national destruction, we come to the nation's story of origin. There in the small plates we find the deepest and richest expansion of the whole covenantal story, and that concludes the record. To rephrase a scripture, the last shall be the middle, and the middle shall be the last.

Encountering the Book of Mormon in this sequence highlights both of our two themes, covenant and inheritance. Starting in Mosiah, the word "covenant" means any number of specific promises in any number of situations but seldom if ever refers to *the* Book of Mormon covenant we discussed earlier. The word "covenant" takes on this meaning only when the voice of the Lord pierces through the darkness in 3 Nephi 10. Upon the Lord's crucifixion in Jerusalem, massive destruction and darkness beset the Book of Mormon peoples. After the earth stilled and the lightning stopped, after homes collapsed and fires burned out, the survivors sat in shock. Then a voice from heaven addressed them in the dark and reminded them of the covenant made to their fathers (see 3 Ne. 10:7).

The idea of covenants made to the fathers bookends the rest of the Book of Mormon when it is read in dictation order. It comes from the heavenly voice in 3 Nephi, and it comes again as a chorus at the end of the small books. The writers of these small books self-consciously understand themselves to be carrying the record forward until it can reach the prophesied remnant in the latter days. They anticipate that time. In dictation order, then, from Christ's visit through the rest of 3 Nephi, Mormon, Ether, and Moroni and into the small plates, the word "covenant" focuses always on *the* Book of Mormon covenant, a subset of the Abrahamic covenant which promises that a record will go to a remnant of the house of Israel in the latter days. Dictation order circles us back to finish with the small plates. As Joseph Spencer points out in this series' volume on 1 Nephi, these small plates were designed to highlight the "more sacred things," namely, the covenant discussed in the Isaiah chapters of 2 Nephi (1 Ne. 19:5). Between Nephi's Isaiah chapters and Jacob's olive tree allegory, and finally with Enos's wrestle that secures anew the promise of the covenant, it is clear that Mormon's placement of the small plates at the end of the book spotlights the covenant.

Dictation order shines a spotlight on the Book of Mormon covenant, but let's linger a moment to set the whole covenantal stage, of which this is only a part. There are individual covenants we make through ordinances such as baptism and the temple endowment. The *mise en scène* here, though, is not individual covenants but collective ones, like the Abrahamic covenant found in the Old Testament. God promised Abraham and Sarah that in their posterity "shall all the nations of the earth be blessed" (Genesis 22:18). Ultimately, the scope of the collective covenant is all the world. If the Abrahamic covenant covers the whole world and the entire stage, so to speak, then a portion of the set scenery is the covenant to the house of Israel (see Gen. 35:9–15). The Book of Mormon covenant then fastens our gaze with urgent precision onto specific prophecies (redemption for Lamanites via the Nephite record) for a specific people (the remnant) in a specific place (the New World) at a specific time (the dispensation of the latter days). It details the workings of the Abrahamic covenant in a Restoration context. Even with this focus, the Book of Mormon covenant touches the entire world through its intended audiences: the remnant, the Jews, the Gentiles, and the house of Israel (see Book of Mormon title page). Just as Jacob, renamed Israel, received a restatement of the Abrahamic covenant tailored to his family and descendants, the Book of Mormon fathers Lehi, Nephi, Jacob, and Enos receive a restatement of the Abrahamic covenant modulated for them. As a specific subset of the earlier covenants, the Book of Mormon covenant knits us together and to those ancient, encompassing promises.

If placing the small plates at the end of Mormon's record emphasizes the Book of Mormon covenant, it's no surprise that in this series each author writing on scripture from the small plates (1 Nephi, 2 Nephi, Jacob, and the short books) demonstrates how the Book of Mormon covenant is central to the message of the individual books. Joseph Spencer shows how Nephi's understanding of the covenant saturates his visions and scripture reading and structures his entire record.[3] In 2 Nephi, Terryl Givens identifies a "new, reformulated covenantal narrative" that grows out of the old covenant.[4] And Deidre Green connects Jacob's focus on relationships to the covenant's relevance to Jacob's audience. She observes, "God's covenant with Israel will not be fulfilled if those within the covenant isolate themselves from others. The tame olive trees that represent Israel (Jacob 6:1) cannot flourish or even survive without the new life introduced by the wild branches."[5] From each author's perspective, the covenant remains in the spotlight.

In this covenantal context, how do these small books of Enos, Jarom, and Omni work as an ending to the Book of Mormon? In a word: inheritance. With a clear view of the plates being passed down through family lines, these books connect the idea of covenant to family. As the plates move—one family member and one generation at a time—they inch closer to fulfilling the covenant, that is, to bringing the record to the descendants of Lehi and Sariah's family in the latter days. Authors of these small books, with a variety of temperaments and talents, contribute over centuries to link their family across dispensations. This diverse cast of characters also draws attention to the impact of family dynamics. We trace each writer's inheritance from the previous generation, as we will see later in more detail. But these books also show that what began as a family feud between Nephi and Laman fully hardened into national rifts and regular war. The fault lines between brothers weren't repaired during their lifetimes, and as the successive generations march on, the conflict ceases to be personal, and contention becomes a way of life. Enos still seems to harbor frustration and a sense of injustice about the Lamanites' behavior, writing of their "evil nature" and "filthiness" (Enos 1:20). But Abinadom, four generations later, speaks dispassionately about "much war and contention," matter-of-factly informing the reader, "I, with my own sword, have taken the lives of many of the Lamanites in the defence of my brethren" (Omni 1:10). What were once serious disagreements between brothers metastasized into habitual political violence.

If we read in dictation order, the small plates connect the chronological end of the Lehite tale to its beginnings. Following Mormon and Moroni's writings, the small plates come on the heels of the Nephites' destruction. In the wake of devastation, we are returned to Laman and Nephi and the family relationships that set it all in motion. Juxtaposing ultimate ruin with the brothers' interactions invites us to consider how far unresolved family discord can reach. In this context, the ingredients of the Nephites' demise are visible throughout the small plates. After Nephi and Jacob's longer books, the time that remains is foreshortened in these small books. (Amaleki remarks that the "plates are full" in Omni 1:30.) Enos, Jarom, and Omni point to the only hope for the family's redemption: the future remnant. These books constitute the end of this first family's spiritual record. Compared to the visions and miracles recounted by Nephi and Jacob, the small books can seem like a fade-out. But the authors of Enos, Jarom, and Omni were doing exactly what the prophecies and covenants instructed them to do; they were ensuring that the plates would survive into the future and reach their intended readers. And these writers are acutely aware of their readers. Enos addresses them directly, "I will tell you of the wrestle which I had" (Enos 1:2). Jarom says outright, "these things are written for the intent of the benefit of our brethren the Lamanites," (Jarom 1:2). Omni writes, "I would that ye should know," and Amaleki begins, "Behold, I will speak unto you," and closes, "I would that ye should come unto Christ" (Omni 1:2, 12, 26). These writers gazed centuries into the future, breaking the fourth wall to speak directly to the remnant.

Dictation order points to the anguish and losses that can occur within family. But it also offers hope that families can be reclaimed, even after they have been destroyed. That seems to be the last message Mormon hoped readers would encounter, and it is unfolded in rapid fashion in the small books of Enos, Jarom, and Omni. What is developed in the small plates is the covenant for Lehi and Sariah's family. It tells the story of how threats to that covenant originated in their family. But it also demonstrates that the renewal of the covenant will come through their family, and it will be fulfilled in spite of the family's failures. This is the big, good news of the Book of Mormon, perhaps its final message. And it is laid bare in these itty bitty books.

1

Enos

Enos feels like a friend. From the start he chats directly with the reader, interrupting himself twice in the first verse, and, in verse 2, writing as though he is looking straight at you: "I will tell you of the wrestle which I had before God" (Enos 1:2). Then he launches into a hunting story. We might say that Enos is someone you could have a root beer with.

He is also, of course, a prophet and a Book of Mormon author. About two-thirds of his short book describes a prayer or series of prayers, and the balance tells what he did in consequence of the answers he received. You probably know the story. Enos's "soul hungered" (Enos 1:4), so he started to pray, and he kept praying. He prays first for his own welfare; then for that of his people, the Nephites; and finally for the Lamanites. God eventually promises that in the future he will remember his covenant to redeem this branch of the house of Israel. It is worth noting that although Enos introduces the story of his long prayer with, "I will tell you of the wrestle which I had before God, before I received a remission of my sins," only three verses into the story Enos hears "thy sins are forgiven thee" (Enos 1:2, 5). Did this wrestle deserve a mere three verses? Perhaps Enos's "wrestle" is not the first prayer he describes. Perhaps it comes later. In the middle portion of his narrative, verses 9 through 15, Enos tells of pouring out his "whole soul," "struggling in the spirit," praying with "many long strugglings," praying and laboring "with all diligence," and crying unto God "continually." This sounds more like wrestling than the what we see in the early verses of his account. These words also don't sound like a one-time, one-day-only event. Rather, Enos presents a process that unfolded over time—maybe days, weeks, or even years.

I propose that Enos's wrestle and its consequences filled his whole life and whole book. This shouldn't surprise us; the transformation and promises in the story of Enos's wrestle epitomize the project of the Book of Mormon, which was "written to the Lamanites" (title page). The Book of Mormon is intended to point them to Jesus and to covenants that bind everyone to the house of Israel and thus to salvation. These are the ramifications of Enos's wrestle. The sequence of when forgiveness and emphasis on the covenant are found in Enos's account imply a few things. First, since most of the story comes after Enos is forgiven, as we have noted, it appears that individual forgiveness can come early in a spiritual journey. Enos said that his wrestle came before he received a remission of his sins. Thus, being forgiven of his sins early on was not necessarily the same thing as the remission of his sins (Enos 1:2). Second, once Enos is forgiven and made whole, the Lord instructs him to "go to" (Enos 1:8), and Enos reports that he "went about...prophesying of things to come, and testifying of the things which I had heard and seen" (Enos 1:19). More specifically, he, with others, "did seek diligently to restore the Lamanites unto the true faith in God" (Enos 1:20). Enos shows that being forgiven and entering a covenant are followed by lots and lots of work. Finally, as will become clearer, we can be forgiven, and we can receive beautiful covenants, even though our weaknesses and blind spots may not go away. They may persist and even be dangerous and painful to us and to others.

Despite the large-scale effects of Enos's wrestle, it

feels personal because Enos is personable. Underlying his accessible and familiar narrative, however, Enos keenly feels his responsibility for the plates. Behind his inviting tone are family expectations, covenant obligations, and scriptural allusions that emphasize the gravity of Enos's experience. This blend of consequence and approachability gives his story its appeal. Enos is a spiritual Everyman who experiences the miracle of being known, heard, and forgiven by the Savior of the world. And in his struggles to understand and draw near to God, his prayer becomes woven into God's covenant, poised to reach countless people beyond Enos's personal sphere of influence. Many of us have experienced bone-deep longing and sought God in wrestles of our own, and some have also tasted the sublime sweetness of forgiveness and being enfolded by the love of the Lord. Many of us have also tasted the bitterness and weariness of trying and failing to live in love with our fellows. Whether we are struggling and hungry, whole and at rest, or somewhere in between, Enos's story speaks to us on an individual level. It may also include far broader consequences.

who is Enos?

Enos is a grandson of Lehi and Sariah and a nephew to Laman, Lemuel, Sam, Nephi, Joseph, and their sisters, unnamed in the text. He is also the first Book of

Mormon author who did not know Lehi or Nephi personally. For all the intimacy of his introduction, we don't know very much about him or his relationships. If we were to sit down for a friendly repast with Enos, we might make conversation by asking him about his family life, because what we do know implies an unusual arrangement.

Jacob says he inherited the plates from Nephi fifty-five years after Lehi and Sariah left Jerusalem, and Enos says he finished his record 179 years after that founding journey (see Jacob 1:1, Enos 1:25).[1] To imagine what this means, picture the following: Let's say you had grandparents who immigrated to the United States in 1841 along with your aunts and uncles already grown. Your father was then born after they arrived, making him a young man during the American Civil War. But only now, in 2020, are you the same age that Enos was at the end of his record. For such timing to work, both Jacob and Enos would had to have lived very long lives. How well did they know each other? Jacob says he instructed Enos about caring for the plates (see Enos 1:1, 3; Jacob 7:27), and Enos says he was born early enough to have "often heard [his] father speak," but these exchanges almost certainly happened while Enos was a child. His extremely aged father must have died when Enos was still quite young. What was Enos's mother like? She is not mentioned in the text, but she would have needed to be much younger than Jacob and was likely present for more (probably much more) of Enos's early years than Jacob was.

Besides teaching him language and the scriptures, Jacob may also have named Enos after Enos of the Old Testament—the son of Seth, nephew to Cain and Abel, and grandson to Adam. After Abel was killed and Cain disinherited, Seth received the birthright and the priesthood from his father and then passed it to his son, Enos (Gen. 4:25–26, 5:1–11). Enos-son-of-Seth was, therefore, a nephew who inherited responsibilities that had first gone to his uncle and then to his father. Perhaps Jacob-son-of-Lehi, reflecting on the priestly assignment and stewardship of the small plates from Nephi, saw a similarity and, like Seth, named his son Enos.

We can tease out further information about Enos and his family based on how he presents himself and how he responds to the writings of Nephi and Jacob. Enos styles himself a hunter, like Nephi (see 1 Ne 16:14–32), and echoes Nephi's well-known introduction with "I, Enos" (see 1 Ne 1:1, Enos 1:1). He also acknowledges the legacy of learning from his father, as we have seen, and this follows Nephi's model ("goodly parents") but also points to Enos's inheritance from Jacob. Following Nephi and Jacob, Enos is a prophet, but he's no founder of a dispensation like Nephi. Rather, Enos operates within an existing religious structure that includes priests, the Law of Moses, a temple, and sacrifices (see 2 Ne. 5:16, 26, 2 Ne. 6:2, Jacob 2:2, 11, Jacob 4:5). His own father, Jacob, was a priest and seems to have been very involved in temple worship and administration (see Jacob 1:17–18; 2:2–3, 11). Although Enos comes from the most prominent family of the Lehite people, he, like his father, does not seem to be in society's spotlight (notice that Sherem seems to have had trouble finding Jacob) (see Jacob 7:3, 6). When the monarchy continues after the death of Nephi, Jacob and his line don't inherit the throne but remain in priestly roles.[2] Perhaps most importantly for our present purposes, though, Enos learns to read and write from his father and had access to ancient and recent scriptures, including Nephi's small plates.

Enos reads those scriptures and thinks about Nephi and Jacob's teachings. His seeking is prompted by "the words which I had often heard my father speak concerning eternal life" (Enos 1:3). Jacob taught that the Lamanites were "more righteous" than his Nephite audience because of how Lamanite wives and husbands loved each other and how parents loved their children. Jacob further asserted that this love alone would prevent the Lamanites' destruction (Jacob 3:5–7).[3] Surely Jacob's championing of the Lamanites contributed to Enos's care for them in his prayer.

The fact that Enos prayed is also probably at least partly due to Nephi's preaching. In the face of soul-hunger like Enos's, Nephi takes prayer to be the clear path: "And now, my beloved brethren, . . . it grieveth me that I must speak concerning this thing. For if ye would hearken unto the Spirit which teacheth a man to pray, ye would know that ye must pray" (2 Ne. 32:8). Further, Nephi urges, "ye must pray always, and not faint" and "pray unto the Father in the name of Christ, that he will consecrate thy performance unto thee, that thy performance may be for the welfare of thy soul" (2 Ne. 32:9). Enos does just as Nephi instructs. His "soul hungered," he "cried . . . in mighty prayer and supplication for [his] own soul" (Enos 1:4), and his effort was consecrated. As double heir of Nephi and Jacob, Enos functions like a third witness of God's covenant regarding the descendants of Lehi and Sariah. The promises made to Nephi that "in the last days" his words would be "of great worth" to his "own people" (2 Ne. 25:8) and that "the remnant of our seed [will] know concerning us" (2 Ne. 30:4) are precisely the outcome of Enos's prayer. God's response to Enos restates and condenses these promises into their most clear and concise form.

Enos also echoes older scriptural traditions. Perhaps most pointedly, in calling his experience a "wrestle," he invokes the experience of the patriarch Jacob whose name was changed to "Israel" in consequence of a wrestle (see Gen. 32:24–30). Enos calls his father a "just man," echoing the description of Noah, who "was a just man and perfect in his generations," perhaps implying that like a son of Noah, he, Enos, is a key link in the priesthood chain on the earth (Enos 1:1; Gen. 6:9). As we will see, the phrase "joy of the saints" has Old Testament connections, too (Enos 1:3). Further, Enos writes that he prayed "all the day long," a phrase that merits some discussion (Enos 1:4). Nearly a third of the uses of this phrase in scripture occur in the Psalms. Perhaps in describing the prayer this way, Enos alludes to a familiar genre of sacred writing. Closer to Enos's own time, though, the phrase also appears in Jacob's version of the allegory of the olive tree. When the season for work nears completion and the trees have not been saved, the Lord of the vineyard despairs, "I have stretched forth mine hand almost all the day long, and the end draweth nigh" (Jacob 5:47). Here the critical addition of "almost" to "all the day long" allows the servant to implore the lord of the vineyard to "spare it a little longer" (Jacob 5:50). They finish out the day by returning scattered branches to their home tree. This return of branches is, of course, the subject of the promise that Enos obtains in prayer—a record of the Nephites will be returned to the Lamanites, and it will help graft the Lamanites back into the covenant tree. Jacob also uses "all the day long" in his commentary on the allegory, but he uses it to describe not human searching, but God's constant outreach for and nourishment of the children of Israel (see Jacob 6:4, 7). Enos had a long time to prepare his contribution to the small plates. Being steeped in scripture, his words reflect the language of prior prophets.

Enos's attention to scripture helps us understand how praying for his own soul in the present leads to praying for a covenant for Lamanites far in the future.

Enos's orientation toward the covenant started before the prayer ever began. He remembers the words of Jacob, specifically about "eternal life, and the joy of the saints" (Enos 1:3). ☞ The only place in the Old Testament that explicitly pairs "joy" and "saints" is Psalm 132. With temple-like overtones, this psalm tells of an incremental ascent to the Lord and of creating Zion: "Let thy priests be clothed with righteousness; and let thy saints shout for joy" (Psalm 132:9), followed some verses later with the Lord declaring that he "will also clothe [Zion's] priests with salvation: and her saints shall shout aloud for joy" (Psalm 132:16). In between these portrayals of joyful shouting, God promises, "If thy children will keep my covenant and my testimony that I shall teach them, their children shall also sit upon thy throne for evermore" (Psalm 132:12). The salvation of posterity is the same assurance that Enos seeks from God for the Nephites and the Lamanites. The only other scripture in our canon that specifically discusses the joy of the saints is D&C 109:80, the conclusion of the Kirtland Temple dedicatory prayer. This Restoration scripture also yearns for a time when the church will be "clothed with salvation, and thy saints shout aloud for joy." The references in Psalms and in the Doctrine and Covenants tie the "joy of the saints" to audible shouts of joy and to clothing for holy ritual. In other words, the "joy of the saints" connects to covenants and temple worship. When Enos thinks on his father's words about "the joy of the saints," he evokes a scriptural tradition of covenants made to groups of people separated by time but joined by God's promises.

☞ The idea that Enos remembered comes from the original manuscript, which reads somewhat differently from our current version: "Behold, I went to hunt beasts in the forest, and I *remembered* the words which I had often heard my father speak concerning eternal life, and the joy of the saints; and the words of my father sunk deep into my heart" (Enos 1:3, emphasis added).

kenosis

Enos's prayer combines his own spiritual yearning with his reflections on God's promises to such groups joined by covenants but separated by time. In this way, Enos's story typifies the pattern of the Book of Mormon as a whole: it appeals to the individual, touching millions of hearts in private, highly personalized ways, and yet its ultimate purpose is to gather peoples and nations. As a self-contained short story with spiritual impact, Enos's account is one that many of us have read and returned to several times. In that vein, I'd like to look at the account Enos gives of his prayer in a few different ways.

First, let's consider an account of the prayer that probably feels familiar: Enos's soul hungers, and, remembering his father's teachings, he turns his feelings to God. God tells Enos that his sins are forgiven, and in response, Enos continues his petition on behalf of, first, the Nephites, and then the Lamanites. In response to these requests, God reaffirms the Book of Mormon covenant that has been promised to Enos's fathers. It's a beautiful scriptural episode of the far-reaching effects of one person's spiritual struggle.

A second look at Enos's prayer reveals some blanks in the story. Enos writes that he cried unto God all the day long and still when night came, but he does not say what he prayed for. Enos tells only that his soul hungered. God's answer to the content of this prayer, whatever it may have been, was to forgive Enos of his sins and assure him that he will be blessed in the future. Anyone who has received such an answer to prayer knows that nothing is sweeter. This still does not clarify, however, the content of Enos's prayer. After hearing that he was forgiven, Enos, understanding the character of God, says that his "guilt was swept away" and simply asks, "Lord, how is it done?" (Enos 1:6–7). God's initial response does not say how, directly. Enos asks how, and

26

God says, "because." God tells Enos, "Because of thy faith in Christ, whom thou hast never before heard nor seen" (Enos 1:8). As if in parallel with the unknown content of Enos's prayer, God informs Enos that he is blessed for his faith in the unheard and unseen Christ. God continues by stating that a confirmation of Christ in the flesh will be deferred still longer: "And many years pass away before he shall manifest himself in the flesh" (Enos 1:8). To this God adds another causal instruction: "wherefore." As if to say that *because* of Enos's faith in an unheard and unseen Christ and *because* it will be many more years before the Christ will show himself in the flesh, Enos is directed, "go to, thy faith hath made thee whole" (Enos 1:8). Here is the answer to Enos's question, "How?" God says, "thy faith hath made thee whole." But God responds to Enos's question only after emphasizing Christ. The sequence of God's response suggests that the takeaway of being made whole is Christ and, subsequently, God's instruction, "go to."

What, then, does it mean to "go to," and what does that have to do with being made whole? These two questions relate, and the framework that makes their relationship clear is *kenosis*.

Kenosis is a concept in theology that means emptying out one's self. The word is derived from the Greek text of Philippians 2:5–11, rendered as follows in the King James Version (KJV):

> 5 Let this mind be in you, which was also in Christ Jesus: 6 Who, being in the form of God, thought it not robbery to be equal with God: 7 But made himself of no reputation, and took upon him the form of a servant, and was made in the likeness of men: 8 And being found in fashion as a man, he humbled himself, and

became obedient unto death, even the death of the cross. 9 Wherefore God also hath highly exalted him, and given him a name which is above every name: 10 That at the name of Jesus every knee should bow, of things in heaven, and things in earth, and things under the earth; 11 And that every tongue should confess that Jesus Christ is Lord, to the glory of God the Father.

The Greek verb *kenóō* (κενόω) is "to empty," and this verb is translated in verse 7 as "to make of no reputation." Other translations of the Bible present the phrase as "made himself nothing" (NIV), "emptied himself" (ESV), and "humbled himself" (NET). What distinguishes this particular emptying is that it is an auto-emptying. To put it grammatically, it is reflexive; the direct object of this emptying is always the self.

The key detail this passage shows, however, is that the outcome of this self-emptying is power. Although it may be counterintuitive, the radical self-emptying described in the first half of the passage *causes* what is found in the second half. Christ emptied himself, or made himself of no reputation, and "as a result" (NET) or "wherefore" (KJV) "God also hath highly exalted him." Self-emptying leads to power in God's economy. Theologians therefore use the word *kenosis* (a noun-form of the verb *kenóō*, which never appears in scripture) to describe this emptying of power that increases power.

What does all of this about self-emptying have to do with Enos? Once we are familiar with *kenosis*, we can see that his prayer takes a similar shape. Enos pours *out his whole soul* unto God on behalf of others. And as a result, God covenants with him, securing blessings for many people in the future. The realization that giving up power increases power prompts us to ask, like Enos, "Lord, how is it done?" We can return to Enos's experience in this light to see what we might learn. 🖝

emptying in Enos

The sequence in Enos's narrative is important. Enos is made whole, and in the next verse he pours out his "whole soul unto God for [the Nephites]" (Enos 1:9). Enos had to be made whole before he could self-empty because self-emptying succeeds from wholeness. This happens in two ways, both because only those who are whole can fully see beyond themselves and their own needs, and because only those who are whole can go through the process of completely emptying. Note that Enos describes his transition to concern for others as a direct consequence of wholeness. The only sentence in his story to start with "now" comes immediately after he hears that he is whole: "Now, it came to pass that when I had heard these words I began to feel a desire for the welfare of my brethren, the Nephites" (Enos 1:9). The word *whole* comes from the same Old English word as *hale* and *heal*, connoting wellness, good health, and healing. This sense of the word lingers in contemporary usage of *wholesome*. But apparently the word *whole* does not signify the end of hunger. The episode begins with Enos detailing the hunger of his soul. Hunger signals the need to care for our own bodies and keep them alive. Wholeness, even with its connotations of health, does not change that need, because after Enos is whole, he continues to want with a longing that is redirected. His hunger transforms into desire on behalf of others— to care for them, their lives, and their welfare. The experience suggests that being made whole does not retire us from care. Instead, it expands and reorients care in

🖝 Kenosis also helps us understand Jacob's relationship to Christ. See Deidre Nicole Green's volume on Jacob in this series (Ch.2).

29

new, salvific directions. Being whole points us to seek wholeness and healing for others.

Only that which is whole or complete can fully empty itself. Being whole is a necessary precondition of emptying in this saving, glorifying way. In Enos's account, as we've seen, he writes these activities back-to-back—his soul was made whole, and then he poured his whole soul out (see Enos 1:8–9). In what sounds like a tongue-twister, Enos could not pour out his whole soul until his soul was whole, but we should be careful to not be too easily content with a tidy turn of phrase. Self-emptying can be painful and dangerous. It's in some sense like giving birth. A mother must be full of a "whole" child and then completely emptied of that child for mother and child to have a chance at success. Because the child's success is so inextricably connected to her body and physical processes, the mother is wholly vulnerable to permanent damage or death. Yet she must be emptied if the child will live. Emptying must be complete. That is how human physical life happens. In a spiritual parallel, Enos "pour[s] out [his] whole soul unto God for [the Nephites]" and is "struggling in the spirit" on their behalf (Enos 1:9–10). And, God assures, the stakes are real.

So far, then, the process goes like this: being whole generates self-emptying, and self-emptying catalyzes focused, complete commitment to the life and welfare of specific people for whom we pour ourselves out. This is no theoretical idea of love, so undefined that we can hide behind its abstraction. This is loving real people with real consequences and costs, even if we do not know these real people right now. They may live in another time or in totally different circumstances than we do. Enos's prayer began with those familiar to him but ultimately turned to people he didn't know and who would live thousands of years in the future. They became real enough for Enos that he labored to secure a

30

divine covenant from God on their behalf. Enos's view of the recipients of the record may have been like Moroni's when he tells readers, "Jesus Christ hath shown you unto me, and I know your doing" (Mormon 8:35). When God makes us whole and then exhorts us to "go to," one outcome is that it reveals others to us. In the course of emptying our souls, others and their lives and realities come into sharp focus, even alarmingly so. Still more startling, not only are others revealed to us with all their specific needs, but such a process can also reveal how entirely we need them, these people whom we previously did not know.

A brief detour here can help us appreciate how we rely on others who are physically and/or temporally distant from us. A closer look at the relationship between the Nephites of Enos's time and those who receive the Book of Mormon in the last days shows how these two groups need each other, even though they are more than two millennia apart. After Enos empties himself to God for the Nephites' benefit, note that God offers no guaranteed blessing. The Nephites will be blessed only to the degree that they keep the commandments. God thus concludes on a foreboding note: "wherefore, I will visit thy brethren according as I have said; and their transgressions will I bring down with sorrow upon their own heads" (Enos 1:10). These terms and conditions seem to be foregone conclusions: the Nephites will transgress, and they will reap sorrow for it. Now, we should note that this declaration of condemnation presages another one like it in the latter days. Over 2,300 years after his exchange with Enos, God tells Joseph Smith, "vanity and unbelief have brought the whole church under condemnation," and "they shall remain under this condemnation until they repent and remember the new covenant, even the Book of Mormon" (D&C 84:55, 57).

What connects these two passages? In both, the pronounced punishment is rooted to the covenant in a "holy land." This phrase, "holy land," shows up only three times in the scriptural canon, and these are the only two places in Restoration scripture.[4] The two texts seem to be related. God tells Enos that he has given the people this land, "and it is a holy land" that God won't curse except "for the cause of iniquity" (Enos 1:10). In the revelation to Joseph Smith, God also links the need for keeping the covenant to preserving this same holy land. He declares condemnation on the children of Zion, emphasizing that it falls on all of us, "until they repent and remember the new covenant, even the Book of Mormon" (D&C 84:57). The connection seems clear, but the contrast between the passages is important, too. In Enos's time, the land's holy status required that its occupants be righteous. Now, in the latter days, there's an additional obligation: we must be righteous and remember the new covenant of the Book of Mormon. God warns of the stakes involved in the last days, "there remaineth a scourge and judgment to be poured out" if we do not repent and remember this covenant of the Book of Mormon (D&C 84:58). Do we take this seriously? God censured the church, "even all," because of treating this particular covenant too lightly (D&C 84:56). Have we repented sufficiently, or is this reproof still in force?

Perhaps our condemnation today is directly tied to the promises God made to Enos. God covenanted that he would insist on righteousness in the land and that he would get this record to the descendants of Lehi and Sariah. What happens if the occupants of the land can't be relied on to fulfill that covenant? What if they're not righteous enough to bring the Book of Mormon to its intended recipients? This scenario is the reason God gives for pouring out scourge and judgment on his people: "For shall the children of the kingdom pollute my holy land? Verily, I say unto you, Nay" (D&C 84:59). Hindsight shows that God has made good on that promise to pour out judgment. He tells Enos as much, confirming the Nephites' destruction: "Wherefore, I will visit thy brethren according as I have said; and their transgressions will I bring down with sorrow upon their own heads" (Enos 1:10). No longer dealing in contingencies, God assures that the Nephites will be visited with sorrow. In the revelation to Joseph Smith, God similarly affirms that repentance is required, otherwise a scourge remains for the church (see D&C 84:57–58). In other words, the Nephites were destroyed. What will happen to us?

With these parallels between the Nephites' and our latter-day condemnation in mind, let's return to Enos's experience to see how we come to need people who seem so far away. When God informs Enos that the Nephites will be destroyed because of their transgressions, it's surprising that Enos's response isn't grief or anger. Rather, "[his] faith began to be unshaken in the Lord" (Enos 1:11). Does Enos not understand? I venture that he comprehends his relationship and the Nephites' relationship to the Lamanites with new clarity. He realizes that since the Nephites cannot be relied on to stay righteous by themselves, they will need the Lamanites to rejuvenate the covenant. That is, if Lehi and Sariah's children are to be re-grafted into the family tree, it will happen through the descendants of the Lamanites—the same Lamanites against whom Enos's people frequently fought wars. When Enos understands that the Nephites will be destroyed, he realizes that the Lamanites will be the select remnant of Israel. So Enos's newfound clarity manifests itself as faith, hope, and charity for the Lamanites. He sees that the Nephites—his posterity—will be destroyed and that the Lamanites will be distanced from the covenant, but the Lamanites will survive. He sees that the Nephites depend on the Lamanites for their return to the covenant and renewed connection to the house of Israel. He sees, as Paul does on a different continent half a millennium later, that "the eye cannot say unto the hand, I have no need of thee" (1 Cor. 12:21). The Nephite "eyes" may have seen, but it will be the Lamanite "hands" that receive the record in the last days. The whole body of Christ will be reconstituted.

Enos sees that in the body of Christ the eye does need the hand, and Lehi and Sariah's family do need the Lamanites after all. His perception of the Lamanites transforms, along with his faith. His faith, he says, begins to be unshaken; that is, perhaps his faith becomes grounded in the awareness of God's love, attentiveness, and promises to all his children, even the Nephites' enemies. With this reframing, Enos finds faith strong enough to see redemption for the Lamanites but also strong enough to see his own need for the Lamanites' spiritual leadership and success. The two transformations are connected. From Enos's vantage point, with his faith beginning to be unshaken, the Lamanites can't be mere one-dimensional antagonists. They can't be reduced to a caricature of bad neighbors or difficult relatives who must be put up with. Instead, they are and must be family. Enos prays for them as such, "with many long strugglings for my *brethren*, the Lamanites" (Enos 1:11, emphasis added). In the previous phase of his prayer Enos refers to the Nephites as "my brethren"; after the revelation of the Nephites' destruction, he counts the Lamanites as his brethren as well. This is the revelation and power of self-emptying or *kenosis*. Loving people, even those unseen or far away—even our enemies—becomes real and essential.[5]

In the course of his prayers, Enos comes to understand the networked interdependence of God's covenant with the house of Israel. As in the allegory of the olive tree, any one tree's success or failure affects the wellbeing and flourishing of all the other trees. In fact, echoing the same allegory (where "go to" is the instruction given to the last servants working in the vineyard), God instructs Enos to "go to" near the beginning of the wrestle, inviting him to work (see Jacob 5:71). And what follows is a lot of work. Enos pours out his whole soul, struggles in the spirit, prays with many long strugglings, labors with all diligence, and cries unto God continually (see Enos 1:9–12, 15). Self-emptying is beautiful and redemptive. It reveals others to us as whole people and fellow members of the body of Christ. And self-emptying is also an enormous amount of work. It's more like mining than like knocking over a pitcher of water. The journey from focusing on ourselves to emptying ourselves in a godly way is demanding and rarely direct.

During what remains of the prayer, Enos gradually hones his labors and desires for the Lamanites to match the shape of the promises God has already made to Enos's fathers. When God assures Enos, "I will grant unto thee according to thy desires," those desires turn out to be precisely focused on the covenant the Lord has already made regarding the Lamanites (Enos 1:12). Enos explains that his desire of God was "that if it should so be, that my people, the Nephites, should fall into transgression, and by any means be destroyed, and the Lamanites should not be destroyed, that the Lord God would preserve a record of my people, the Nephites . . . that it might be brought forth at some future day unto the Lamanites" (Enos 1:13). Look at the contigencies pile up in Enos's request. God promises to grant Enos's desires, which turn out to be remarkably detailed and complicated. The many layers that undergird the outcome of Enos's prayers for the Lamanites illustrate how much thought, effort, and communication went into it. Self-emptying is work.

Enos's work is inspiring, but we should pause for a moment to clarify what self-emptying is not. It isn't masochistic. God isn't a doormat, nor should we be. And anyway, no doctrine is true in a vacuum. We can only understand a truth, and thus, it can only be fully true, in the context of other revealed truths. We must therefore understand self-emptying side by side with stewardship and charity and divine identity and agency and all the rest. And so the fact that Enos poured himself out for the Lamanites and was blessed for it in no way means that we should stay with an abusive spouse. It doesn't mean that we should accommodate unhealthy relationships or inappropriate behaviors from others. It doesn't mean that cruelty gets a pass, or that people under systemic oppression have to sit there and take it. It's true that Enos obtained the covenant from God once he had self-emptied and redirected his concerns and desires to others' benefit. But it's also true—and of critical importance—that he self-emptied and redirected his concern only after his own soul was whole. Some are in a place where they must learn to exercise faith and give up power. Others are in a place where they must learn to exercise faith and accept God's power and willingness to heal them, to reveal and restore their own worth. Over the long course of life, eternity, and exaltation, all of us certainly will need to learn and exercise faith in both of these ways.

So self-emptying enables salvation but casting pearls before swine does not. How, then, do we differentiate salvific from swine-like circumstances? Self-emptying reveals others to us as real and worthy people—their wonderfulness, their warts, their wisdom, their what-on-earth-were-they-thinking, and everything else. Coming to see things so clearly requires a lot of work, but this is only the first half of things. When God reveals others to us, that inspired insight also summons us to work from our newfound perspective. This relationship between God revealing others to us and the work that attends that revelation is real. It's worth reflecting further on what our work of loving looks like. Much of Enos's struggle may have been the internal work of shifting his view of the Lamanites, no longer seeing them as metaphoric swine, because he could see them as heirs and heralds of salvation. Woven into Enos's explanations of his wrestle are comments about the Lamanites. Twice he emphasizes that the Nephites' efforts to bring them back to the faith "were vain," and twice he tells how the Lamanites, in wrath, sought to "destroy" the Nephites and their records (Enos 1:14, 20). He also remarks that he witnessed wars—more than one—between the Nephites and Lamanites during his lifetime (see Enos 1:24). By Enos's day, Nephites and Lamanites were entrenched enemies.

Let's think about the present. Who feels like your enemy? The person who makes fun of your child? The unreasonable neighbor? An ex? A co-worker out to get you? The one who lies and still gets prominent church callings? Or, who as a group seems to be against everything you stand for? Socialists? Democrats? Republicans? Libertarians? Pro-choice advocates? Pro-lifers? Environmentalists? Feminists? Preppers? Neo-Nazis? Globalists? Pornographers? Suburban racists? To put it in Mormon's terms, which manner of -ites? Whoever they are and in whatever ways they are dangerous or destructive, would you engage in a spiritual wrestle over a long period of time to secure blessings for them and their descendants? Enos's experience suggests that the same people we view as antithetical to our ideals could ultimately play a key role in our salvation, to say nothing of the commandments to love our neighbor, judge not, and pray for our enemies.

Enos's effort was diligent and determined enough to result not just in God giving him comfort but also in granting his desires for a confirmed covenant on behalf of the Lamanites and their posterity. Presumably, God doesn't hand out covenants for entire peoples willy-nilly. Such promises don't usually go to the half-hearted petitioner. We have to assume that Enos really had come to see his own dependence on the Lamanites for the survival of their entire family and that his dogged praying and struggling grew out of having come to truly want those blessings for the Lamanites.

We find ourselves in a similar position today. Returning to Doctrine & Covenants 84, God told Joseph Smith that the whole church is under condemnation—all of us—for not taking the covenant of the Book of Mormon seriously enough. It turns out that, like Enos, we need the remnant to whom the Book of Mormon is addressed. We need Lehi and Sariah's latter-day posterity to receive it and recognize their place in the covenant, as so many prophets explain (see title page; 1 Ne. 14, 15; 2 Ne. 3, 9; 3 Ne. 21; Morm. 5 for examples). Without them, we face a scourge and judgment, and the condemnation remains. We need others, including those who, considering the regular orbits of our daily lives, seem unrelated to us. And so we, too, have work to do. Are we ready to pour out our whole souls? Are we ready for *kenosis*? Are we ready for the revelation of God's children to us and the work that will undoubtedly accompany it? This path requires a multiplicity of spiritual approaches. It is offering not just our coat but our cloak also (see Matt. 5:40). It is giving what we can and when we cannot give, thinking, "I give not because I have not, but if I had I would give" (Mosiah 4:24). It is mourning with those who mourn and comforting those who stand in need of comfort (see

Mosiah 18:9). It is the kind of personalized, effortful love of Joseph Smith reconciling with William W. Phelps after a bitter separation, "Come on dear Brother since the war is past, For friends at first are friends again at last."[6]

These examples, and the example of Enos himself, suggest that self-emptying isn't typically a team sport. But what would a whole community of such individuals look like? Perhaps it would look like the Anti-Nephi-Lehies burying their weapons and preferring death to war (Alma 24). Perhaps it would look like the United Order early in our dispensation, with the Saints attempting to consecrate all they had to the church. Perhaps it would look like Ghanaian disciples in the 1960s and 1970s organizing themselves into branches without priesthood and without baptism, awaiting the day the institutional body of Christ would join itself to them.[7] Undoubtedly, a self-emptying people looks like Zion, where the people are of one heart and one mind, with no poor among them (see Moses 7:18). Can such emptying happen at the communal level? Surely it must, if we are to hope for heaven. And surely it will be messy work getting there.

What, though, is the alternative? From our twenty-first century perspective we have the benefit of seeing the whole of Nephite history, the end from the beginning. The Book of Mormon ends with every last Nephite killed or assimilated beyond recognition. The Mulekites saw, with Coriantumr's death, the extinction of the Jaredites. And mass death is something we know today, too well. A contemporary account shows what is at stake.

Over the course of a few months in 1994, between half a million and one million Rwandans were murdered in pre-planned mass violence. Most were killed face-to-face in their own villages by their own neighbors using personal weapons or farm tools. In hundreds of thousands of instances rape preceded murder. Once the killing was stopped, the survivors and murderers had to confront—beyond grief and trauma and rebuilding—hard questions of justice and retribution. Years later, Paul Kagame, President of Rwanda, said in an interview: "You can't lose one million people in one hundred days without an equal number of perpetrators. But we also can't imprison an entire nation." Because of the sheer number of crimes, Rwandans decided to use local, informal courts with reduced penalties to encourage perpetrators to come forward. The aggrieved were asked to forgive murderers. The murderers were asked to turn themselves in and provide the truth about how survivors' loved ones had died. As we might imagine, this was a horrendously difficult process as known killers were legally rehabilitated and released to return to their towns and villages. Kagame continues:

> It was a huge burden to place on the survivors. And perhaps the burden was too great. One day during a memorial service, I was approached by a survivor. He was very emotional. "Why are you asking us to forgive?" he asked me. "Haven't we suffered enough? We weren't the cause of this problem. Why must we provide the solution?" These were very challenging questions. So I paused for a long time. Then I told him: "I'm very sorry. You are correct. I am asking too much of you. But ... 'Sorry' won't bring back any lives. Only forgiveness can heal this nation. The burden rests with the survivors because they are the only ones with something to give.[8]

This is a harrowing idea. If it is used to shame or blame victims, it is evil. And yet, "something to give" beyond what is reasonable to ask sounds like self-emptying. It sounds like consecration. Ultimately, consecration may be what self-emptying *kenosis* is, requiring our whole souls and a consistent wrestle to seek the kind of relationship with others that God's covenants require. Does it really come down to choosing kenotic forgiveness or total destruction? In the context of eternity, yes. Two factors are at play. First, we don't live alone in the world. We will, therefore, confront the will of others. Second, God insists on preserving agency, for us and for others. God so loved the world that he gave his only begotten son. He lost a third of the hosts of heaven. He made the tree of the knowledge of good and evil available to our first parents. The question is always whether, possessing the gift of agency, we will insist on our will, as Satan did in the council of heaven. Satan's grasping impulse is the inversion of self-emptying's release. Can the choice be so reduced? We hoard our will to ourselves or we self-empty in the service of others. As a poet has said, "We must love one another or die."[9] Seen thus, pouring out our whole souls loses its irrationality. It may still be terrifying, but it is not blind, foolish, or naive. It's necessary, true, and beautiful.

after

The consecrated, self-emptying of *kenosis* is a tall order, and, as Neal A. Maxwell put it, "understandably we tremble inwardly at what may be required."[9] One more look at Enos's story reiterates how weak we are compared to the task at hand, but it also offers, I believe, a source of hope. Enos rightfully serves as an example of diligent devotion to God, his people, and their political enemies, but he has his hang-ups too.

Before approaching Enos's account a third time, we need to look at what he writes after describing his wrestle. As we noted at the beginning of this chapter, Enos's wrestle spans a long time, and even when he finishes his account of his prayers, Enos's wrestle doesn't seem to be entirely resolved. Enos reports that he (re)secures a promise from the Lord that a Nephite record will survive and be a means to save Lamanites in the future. Yet a mere two verses later he writes, "their hatred was fixed," and he doesn't stop there. (Enos 1:20). Enos continues in what sounds increasingly like a rant, heaping criticism upon complaint in such rapid succession that we can hear and feel his utter frustration. Enos writes, "they were led by their evil nature that they became wild, and ferocious, and a blood-thirsty people, full of idolatry and filthiness;" and then he adds derogatory particulars,

> ...feeding upon beasts of prey; dwelling in tents, and wandering about in the wilderness with a short skin girdle about their loins and their heads shaven; and their skill was in the bow, and in the cimeter, and the ax. And many of them did eat nothing save it was raw meat (Enos 1:20).

Hang on. Here we find Lamanites eating raw meat as further evidence of their baseness, but this was the very activity Nephi praised in his family while they journeyed in the wilderness (see 1 Ne. 17:2). Why the double standard? Why the about-face? Enos says his soul rested because he knew that the Lamanites would be saved, but his description of them does not seem to come from a rested soul. Enos seems angry, possibly resentful and disgusted. The failure to reclaim the Lamanites and the Nephite disillusionment with them seems to be complete.

We'll look more closely at these biases and anger, along with their tragic consequences, in the next chapter. For now, this diatribe leaves us with pressing questions: How do we square this disdain for the Lamanites with Enos's obtaining a covenant from God on their behalf? What do we make of this friendly figure who is simultaneously prejudiced? How can God make a covenant with Enos for a people Enos holds in contempt? Doesn't self-emptying require that we see others both clearly and charitably?

Enos turns outward to the welfare of others, but he also retains a focus on his own role in obtaining the Lord's blessings. Several times he refers to the intensity and duration of his "strugglings" or spiritual labor. Enos starts with a "mighty prayer" that lasted "all the day long" and into the night (Enos 1:4), but he also reports "struggling in the spirit," praying "with many long strugglings," that he "prayed and labored with all diligence," and that he cried unto God "continually" (Enos 1:10, 11, 12, 15). As we've already noted, these are praiseworthy efforts on Enos's part, not necessarily something to criticize. Yet they receive quite a bit of emphasis. Enos also highlights how the Lord's responses, blessings, and covenant were given according to his—that is, to Enos's—actions and attributes. He notes that the Lord responded, "I will grant unto thee according to thy desires," and promised "whatsoever thing" Enos asked in faith (Enos 1:12, 15). Enos goes on to emphasize his own role: "And I had faith, and I did cry unto God . . . and he covenanted with me" (Enos 1:16). The directness of Enos's communication with God inspires us; it emboldens us to ask and strengthens our faith that God will answer. Even so, is it possible that at times Enos lost sight of where the power and miracles really come from?

If we go back to the first moment of contact Enos describes in his prayer, we find a window into the mix of his motivations. Early on, a voice came and told Enos that his sins were forgiven and that he would be blessed. Enos assumes the voice is God's, but he makes a psychological detour before experiencing the benefit: "And I, Enos, knew that God could not lie; wherefore, my guilt was swept away" (Enos 1:6). Enos's reaction comes in stages. First he verifies intellectually that, since God cannot lie, the message cannot be false (which is not exactly the same as determining that it is true). After that, his guilt is swept away. This doesn't quite sound like a moment in which Enos is overwhelmed by God's saving power.

It is worth pausing on the phrase, "my guilt was swept away." It isn't found anywhere else in scripture, and this is one of the few scriptural references to sweeping with positive connotations. Most instances refer to sweeping off or destroying a people, often as a result of God's wrath.[11] We've already seen how carefully Enos includes other scriptures in his writing, so it's curious that he would use imagery that connects personal forgiveness with the destruction of a people or nation, a theme that arises later in his prayer. The two prophets Enos imitates—Nephi and Jacob—both write about the ruin of something swept away, specifically in relation to God's covenant with the house of Israel. Nephi quotes Isaiah, saying that the Lord will sweep the remnant "with the besom [or broom] of destruction" (2 Ne. 24:23), and in the olive tree allegory Jacob tells of sweeping out the bad from the house of Israel (Jacob 5:66). So why would Enos allude to God's frightening responses when discussing his own forgiveness? Perhaps it helps draw attention to a particular aspect of his response to that forgiveness.

First, we should note that forgiveness of sins is not the same as removal of guilt. Enos talks about both; a voice told him his sins were forgiven, and then, when he knew God could not lie, his guilt was swept away. What is the difference? At least partly the former is external and spiritual while the latter is internal and psychological. We would all love to not feel guilty, to be sure. But Enos focuses on the cessation of his negative, personal feeling of guilt. He hears the voice, determines that he can trust it, and then his guilt is swept away. It seems here that Enos thinks through his forgiveness more than he feels it. Dislodging and discarding Enos's guilt is not necessarily a mighty change of heart. Contrast Enos's experience with the collective response to King Benjamin's sermon: "they were filled with joy, having received a remission of their sins, and having peace of conscience" (Mosiah 4:3). Or consider Alma the Younger's rejoicing: "I...have been redeemed of the Lord; behold I am born of the Spirit...I am snatched, and my soul is pained no more" (Mosiah 27:24, 29). Every person's conversion is unique, but Enos gestures to the removal of guilt without dwelling on the beauty of grace. It sounds a little more like a therapy session than like sanctification.

Perhaps Enos writes this on purpose as a way of pointing out how, from the beginning, he struggled to get out of his own way. Earlier we noted that when Enos asked "how," the Lord answered, "because." To refresh our memory, that verse reads, "Because of thy faith in Christ, whom thou hast never before heard nor seen. And many years pass away before he shall manifest himself in the flesh; wherefore, go to, thy faith hath made thee whole" (Enos 1:8). Only after dwelling on Christ, his coming, and God's charge to Enos to get to work, only after all of this does God answer the original question and tell Enos that his faith made him whole. The roundabout response highlights where the focus should be—on Christ first, then on the work to do. These two responses take priority. Then, finally, God responds to the question and addresses Enos's faith. The sequence seems to say that yes, Enos's faith is critical and makes a real difference. But it shouldn't be the focus he takes from the experience.

And yet, as we have seen, Enos refers many times to the role of his faith and his desires in obtaining answers to his prayers. After gaining forgiveness for his own sins, Enos is eager to secure blessings for others, but perhaps he occasionally gets the priorities out of order. Perhaps he is tempted to focus on the impact of his faith rather than on Christ. We could read hints of this in Enos's words such as, "my faith began to be unshaken" or "after I had prayed and labored with all diligence, the Lord said unto me: I will grant unto thee according to thy desires, because of thy faith" (Enos 1:11–12). The Lord told Enos, "Whatsoever thing ye shall ask in faith, believing that ye shall receive in the name of Christ, ye shall receive it" (Enos 1:15). But when Enos repeats this promise in his own words, he leaves out the part about Christ: "And I had faith, and I did cry unto God . . . and he covenanted with me" (Enos 1:16). At last, Enos's soul can rest, and he is content with the answers he has received. Then, as if to gently remind Enos that this outcome was not solely his doing, God observes, "Thy fathers have also required of me this thing; and it shall be done unto them according to their faith; for their faith was like unto thine" (Enos 1:18).

Enos has a literary precedent for overemphasizing his own righteousness: Nephi. Joseph Spencer has demonstrated in his volume in this series that Nephi could be distracted by his own spiritual performance at the expense of others' needs. As Spencer puts it, Nephi "prioritized his own promises over those of everyone else" and then "tells the story so as to make readers wonder whether he was ready for what God promised him."[12] Isn't this how Enos writes his account as well? Even after reconfirming the covenant that saves the Lamanites, Enos's feelings toward them leave us wondering if he was ready for that promise. If Enos felt a kinship with Nephi's tendencies, it is no surprise that he adopted Nephi's signature narrative address. Five times he writes, "I, Enos," echoing "I, Nephi" (Enos 1:1, 6, 11, 17, 19). In each case he expresses what he knows, and he models the spiritual care and certainty of Nephi. Maybe he feels solidarity with his uncle who struggled in similar ways to balance spiritual knowledge with self-importance.

Does Enos really have a version of a savior complex? I don't know. We get a sense in these examples that Enos could pivot from heartfelt prayers on behalf of the Lamanites to impassioned contempt for them when he can't save them. But if these textual subtleties are real, I want to give Enos credit for putting them there. He is the one who juxtaposes his prayers for a covenant to bless the Lamanites with his tirade about their depravity. He is the one who echoes Nephi in writing style and spiritual shortcomings. He is the one who, in his final verses, puts away his obsession with Lamanite wickedness and finishes his record and life doing what he can serving the Nephites (see Enos 1:21–27).

When Enos announces that he will tell us about his wrestle, he may have been signaling something larger than the struggle for his own forgiveness and even beyond the renewed covenant. Perhaps Enos is telling us about his wrestle to live up to the love that the covenant requires. Maybe this is why Enos's account is so compelling: in a soup of his own noble and selfish desires, God's will and God's compromises, and the consequences of others' agency, he models the lifelong wrestle to understand and keep covenants.

Why bring up Enos's weaknesses? What does it help? At a minimum, it shows at least two things: first, people are complicated, and second, God can handle it. It's painful to see Enos's blind spots on display. Yet his example—the good and the not-so-good—means that we, too, can do tremendous good in spite of our blind spots. We can receive binding, saving covenants. Our sins can be remitted, even while we are weak in ways that aren't completely apparent to us. We can still do a lot of good and exercise a lot of love. We shouldn't presume that the obviousness of someone's failings and the reality of their goodness are mutually exclusive.

Enos wrestled, struggled, labored, emptied himself, and ultimately blessed the Lamanites over the course of his life, but he wasn't perfect. Neither do we need to be. In a blend of successes and shortcomings, God can reveal Enos to us as real, and we can love him. Enos's wrestle indicates that God can and will give us that revelation for others if we work for it. We can then see their weakness and love them too. As we do, we can, like Enos, look forward "with pleasure" to a place prepared for us in the mansions of our Father and know that we will need each other to get there (Enos 1:27).

2

Jarom

Jarom can be easy to overlook. He doesn't write very much—Amaleki in the book of Omni contributes more words—and his smallest of these already-small books is sandwiched between the beloved story of his father, Enos, and the intriguing societal changes during the four generations in the book of Omni. Jarom is stuck in the middle and doesn't stick out. He kept the plates for fifty-nine years, so it wasn't for lack of time or experience that he didn't write much. He excuses his brevity at both the beginning and the end of his account, saying that the "plates are small" (Jarom 1:2, 14). Maybe the Nephites had lost the technology to make new plates and Jarom is accurately describing the amount of space left. Maybe he's just not into engraving, or maybe spiritual concerns or the covenant aren't his thing. Maybe he represents a period of Nephite apostasy, and we're lucky that he wrote anything at all.

Or maybe Jarom's inconspicuousness is part of his total commitment to the larger purpose of the covenant. In this chapter I invite us to rethink our perceptions of Jarom and understand the significance of what is *not* in his book. To make sense of this, we draw again on the idea of self-emptying or *kenosis* that we discussed in the previous chapter. As we've seen, in the act of self-emptying, Christ "did not regard equality with God as something to be grasped" (Philip. 2:6, NET). In like manner, Jarom does not regard equality with Enos or the other recordkeepers as something to grasp at or prove. He is content to make and keep the record in the way that is needed—to go until he can say "this sufficeth me" (Jarom 1:2). Reading between the lines, Jarom reveals himself as deeply devoted to the covenant that his father secured, and his deference to the needs of the covenant means that he deflects attention away from his own position, revelations, and interests. What he empties or purposefully leaves out doesn't always announce itself. Consequently, we can find Jarom's commitment in his omissions. Sometimes these omissions are selective. In these short books that replay junctures of inheritance over and over, Jarom is also discriminating about what he keeps from his father's legacy and what he lets go. He seems to be intentional about what he will and will not pass down to the next generation. Before diving into what we find in Jarom's text, then, let's take a look at an important omission, something Jarom does not pass down. Jarom is the first writer of the small plates not to use the word "filthiness."

filthiness

The word *filthiness* offers a window into one way that the Nephites developed a bias against the Lamanites. To trace how this word developed, we need to back up to both Nephi's and Jacob's records.

In the Book of Mormon the word *filthy* first comes up in Nephi's (but not Lehi's) vision of the tree of life. The angel tells Nephi that the depths of "the fountain of filthy water which thy father saw" are "the depths of hell" (1 Nephi 12:16). This information comes just after the angel shows Nephi battles between his descendants and the descendants of his brothers several hundred years in the future. When the angel shows Nephi the battles and describes the filthy water as the "depths of hell," the angel also associates the mists of darkness with the "temptations of the devil," and the large and spacious building with the "vain imaginations and the pride of the children of men" (1 Ne. 12:16–19). The angel further explains that the "children of men" are divided by a "great and terrible gulf" that is the word of the justice of God (1 Ne. 12:18).

Although this is what the angel talks about, Nephi experiences it as a kind of voiceover while he watches something else. He recounts, "While the angel spake these words, I beheld and saw that the seed of my brethren did contend against my seed...and because of the pride of my seed, and the temptations of the devil, I beheld that the seed of my brethren did overpower the people of my seed" (1 Ne. 12:19). So, while Nephi hears about what the filthy water, mists of darkness, and large and spacious building mean, he sees his brothers' posterity destroy his own. Notice that Nephi associates two of the three elements from Lehi's dream with his descendants. That is, "because of the pride of [Nephi's] seed" (the large and spacious building), and "the temptations of the devil," (the mists of darkness), "the seed of [Nephi's] brethren did overpower the people of [Nephi's] seed." Nephi watches the slaughter of his people while hearing about these three aspects of the vision, and he also hears the angel assign two of the three aspects to the Nephites as reasons for their downfall.

The third aspect is the filthy water, and it, too, seems to contribute to the downfall of the Nephites. The angel does not explicitly connect it with Lamanites, but it seems that Nephi does. At this point in the narrative Nephi already associates water with Laman and Lemuel. Early in their journey away from Jerusalem, Lehi and Sariah's family pitched their tents, "by the side of a river of water," a river Lehi named "Laman" (1 Ne. 2:6, 8). In Lehi's vision when Lehi is eating from the tree of life, he wants Laman and Lemuel to join the family at the tree. He "cast [his] eyes towards the head of the river" to look for them (1 Ne. 8:17). He sees them, but they don't come. Thus, before Nephi expounds his own vision, he records two scenes that connect Laman to a river. It's not a big leap, then, that in describing his vision he continues to associate Laman with rivers. Nephi sees the seed of his brothers vanquish his descendants in battle and then sees many successive generations of the Lamanites. The angel explains that "these shall dwindle in unbelief" (1 Ne. 12:22), and then Nephi "beheld" that "they became a dark, and loathsome, and a filthy people" (1 Ne. 12:23). Nephi has already established a river as a symbol of Laman. He sees a vision of a "filthy" river, and he links the word "filthy" with Lamanites.

Nephi further entrenches the association of Lamanites with filthiness when he discusses the vision with his brothers. After the vision closes, he returns to his family and finds his brothers disputing over Lehi's teachings. Nephi has a strong emotional response to the situation, though it's not clear what, exactly, Nephi's brothers have done wrong beyond not asking the Lord about their questions. Nephi comments on the hardness of their hearts four times in this brief episode (1 Ne. 15:3–4, 10–11), he considers his afflictions to be "great above all" because he witnessed the end of his people (1 Ne. 15:5), and he takes some time to recover his strength before returning to the conversation (1 Ne. 15:6). Against this backdrop Nephi then unfolds their family's role in the prophecies about the house of Israel. Notice the pronouns: "in the latter days, when *our* seed shall have dwindled in unbelief...then shall the fulness of the gospel of the Messiah come...from the Gentiles unto the remnant of *our* seed—And at that day shall the remnant of *our* seed know...that they are the covenant people of the Lord" (1 Ne. 15:13–14, emphasis added). At this point in the small plates, Laman, Lemuel, and the other brothers (and, presumably, in-laws) could still reasonably imagine that their descendants would all be one people instead of divided into two major groups. There have been disagreements, of course, and brief violence, but, so far, nothing has happened that would make them think that the group would permanently split into warring factions. Nephi, however, has just seen the bloody future reality of his and their descendants' division, and he obscures this part of the prophecies by saying "our seed" rather than "my seed" and "your seed."

When Nephi's brothers ask about the meaning of Lehi's dream, though, the emotional associations of Nephi's own vision apparently resurface. Nephi returns to connecting his brothers to the river and its filthiness. He offers interpretations of the tree of life and the iron rod, urging his brothers with all his soul to hold fast to it and heed the word of God (1 Ne. 15:24–25). But when they ask about the river, the first thing Nephi tells them, even before saying that the river represents hell, is that the river "was filthiness" (1 Ne. 15:27). Then he connects it to the gulf the angel mentioned that divides the wicked from the saints (1 Ne. 15:28), and identifies the river as "a representation of that awful hell . . . prepared for the wicked" (1 Ne. 15:29). As Nephi explains it, the river is more than a place, like a gulf or hell; it is a state of being, a state of filthiness.

As his brothers ask for more details about the finality of God's judgment, Nephi brings up the idea of filthiness multiple times. Specifically, he hammers home that filthiness is excluded from the kingdom of God. Speaking of people approaching the final judgment, Nephi explains, if their works have been filthiness they must needs be filthy; and if they be filthy it must needs be that they cannot dwell in the kingdom of God; if so, the kingdom of God must be filthy also. But...the kingdom of God is not filthy...wherefore there must needs be a place of filthiness prepared for that which is filthy. And there is a place prepared, yea, even that awful hell....Wherefore, the wicked are rejected from the righteous, and also from that tree of life....And thus I spake unto my brethren (1 Ne. 15:33–36).

For our purposes in understanding the word "filthiness," the gist of this lengthy pronouncement is that the filthy cannot be with God, so they must go to that awful hell. What was that awful hell? The river. The river is filthiness and the place prepared for filthiness. It is the separator, or gulf, between the wicked and the righteous. Laman and Lemuel, standing by the river, would not come to the tree. In the vision, Laman and Lemuel chose filthiness. Nephi punctuates this link between his brothers and the filthy river by finishing, "And thus I spake unto my brethren."[1] Within this passage we see one genesis for the Nephite practice of separating from or even rejecting Lamanites. It is explicitly because of their perceived filthiness.[2] Of course, numerous other factors shape the animosity that arises between the groups, but here is an inflection point for how Nephites could associate the specific idea of filthiness with the Lamanites.

The idea of filthiness seems to stick. Years later, Jacob refers to it as though it is a kind of buzz word, like an emotionally fraught label that is especially effective for grabbing the Nephites' attention. Preaching at the temple, Jacob points out, "Behold, the Lamanites your brethren, whom ye hate because of their filthiness and the cursing which hath come upon their skins, are more righteous than you" (Jacob 3:5). In her volume in this series, Deidre Green discusses the racial and othering elements that Jacob addresses in this sermon.[3] Joseph Spencer suggests that we could read this verse with filthiness in scare quotes, as though it is a pejorative label commonly applied to the Lamanites, but which Jacob is using ironically. Paraphrased thus, it would say, "You hate the Lamanites because of their 'filthiness' you so often talk about, but they are more righteous than you."[4] Note also that Jacob talks about filthiness in the same breath as the cursing of the Lamanites' skins. While acknowledging how imprecise it can be to draw cultural inferences across centuries and translations, at this point in Nephite history, the word "filthiness" seems to have taken on racial connotations. Jacob wants to rebuke Nephite sin in the strongest terms (Jacob 2:5–10), so when he addresses the Nephites' "grosser crimes," he may use the charged idea of filthiness for its shock value (Jacob 2:23). Following Spencer's reading, consider this preaching from Jacob again as if the word "filthy" were in scare quotes: "wo, wo, unto you...that are 'filthy' this day before God...and the Lamanites, which are not 'filthy' like unto you...shall possess the land of your inheritance (Jacob 3:3–4, punctuation added).[5] The idea of filthiness that the Nephites commonly associate with the Lamanites is tied to anxiety about who will ultimately possess the land—all ideas that stem from Nephi's vision of a filthy river and a final battle between Nephites and Lamanites.

If Jacob's record shows that the idea of filthiness has settled into Nephite culture as a derogatory signifier for the Lamanites, in Enos we find that, many decades later, the idea is still there. As noted in the previous chapter, when Enos relates how he sees the depravity of the Lamanites, his culminating descriptor is that they are "full of...filthiness" (Enos 1:20). Enos could describe the Lamanites in a variety of ways; he chooses an ethnic slur.

Jarom, however, refrains. Nephi, Jacob, and Enos each apply "filthiness" to the Lamanites, but not Jarom. He leaves it out. His descriptions are more dispassionate, showing simply that the Lamanites do not observe the Nephites' religion. The two reports Jarom makes—that the Lamanites "loved murder and would drink the blood of beasts" (Jarom 1:6)—may simply refer to local religious rituals and explicitly signal that the Lamanites did not follow the Law of Moses, which forbids drinking the blood of animals killed for their meat.[6] Even though by this point the Nephites and Lamanites are established enemies, Jarom stops at this description and avoids adding judgmental commentary.

Jarom is the first author of the small plates who does not call the Lamanites filthy. Although this is a small detail, it aligns with other omissions in Jarom's record. At the beginning of his account, Jarom informs the reader, "I shall not write the things of my prophesying, nor of my revelations.... For have not [my fathers] revealed the plan of salvation?... Yea; and this sufficeth me" (Jarom 1:2). Keeping his eye on what is needed for the record, Jarom is content to leave his spiritual accomplishments unrecorded. His omissions suggest that Jarom is dutiful, generous, and not afraid to empty himself. He quietly sifts his inheritance and carefully passes on a better one. But perhaps we're getting ahead of ourselves. All of this becomes apparent as we get to know Jarom better.

taking prophecy seriously

As Enos's son, Jarom knows of his father's prayers and prophecies about the salvation of the Lamanites via the record of the Nephites. Jarom understands his own contribution to the small plates serves the same purpose: "these things are written for the intent of the benefit of our brethren the Lamanites" (Jarom 1:2). At the same time, Jarom says that the Lamanites "came many times against us, the Nephites, to battle" (Jarom 1:7). He is left to sort out competing interests regarding the prophecies. He cares for the records and their foretold role in blessing the Lamanites' seed, and at the same time his people regularly fend off Lamanite attacks. What, if anything, should he or any of the Nephites be doing to prove faithful to the prophecies of their fathers?

The bulk of Jarom's account, as it turns out, details efforts to keep the Nephites from being destroyed because of wickedness. After introducing himself and his responsibility for the record, Jarom writes that "much should be done among [the Nephites], because of the hardness of their hearts, and the deafness of their ears, and the blindness of their minds, and stiffness of their necks." He connects all of this to the possibility that they could be "swept...off from the face of the land" (Jarom 1:3). In an effort to mitigate the Nephites' susceptibility to wickedness, their leaders adopt severe measures, making the "laws of the land...exceedingly strict," having the "prophets of the Lord...threaten the people of Nephi...that if they did not keep the commandments...they should be destroyed" (Jarom 1:5, 10). These priorities came from the top because, according to Jarom, "our kings and leaders were mighty men in the faith of the Lord; and they taught the people the ways of the Lord" (Jarom 1:7). It wasn't just the political leaders; "the prophets, and the priests, and the teachers, did labor diligently, exhorting with all long-suffering the people to diligence; teaching the law of Moses...persuading them to look forward unto the Messiah" (Jarom 1:11). Jarom maintains that this ministry of "prick[ing] their hearts with the word, continually stirring them up to repentance" is what kept the Nephites "from being destroyed upon the face of the land" (Jarom 1:12).

The Nephites didn't work to survive only by developing spiritual strength. Jarom also paints a picture of civic and technological development. The Nephites "became exceedingly rich" in precious metals, woodworking, buildings, machinery, iron, copper, brass, and steel (Jarom 1:8). They constructed agricultural tools and weapons of war, and Jarom links all of this to their preparation to defend themselves against the Lamanites. In short, during this period, Jarom portrays Nephite leadership as concentrated on prolonging the Nephites' survival partially because of the prophecies of their fathers and partially despite the prophecies that said they would not survive.

Although Jarom's first entry in the small plates was two hundred years after Lehi, Sariah, and company left Jerusalem, Lehi was Jarom's great-grandfather, only three generations removed. Like the person-to-person priesthood ordination outlined elsewhere in scripture, the accounts of Nephi, Jacob, and Enos's prophecies were handed down in person to their respective children, presumably, in many cases, in intimate family settings. The prophecies said that if (or, really, when) the Nephites failed to live in righteousness, they would be wiped off the land. Jarom writes in earnest, and it seems that he and his associates sincerely believe that their lives depend on how well they heed these visions and warnings from their founding fathers.

What is at stake for the Nephites in these beliefs? As Enos's wrestle summarizes, God will not always allow an unrighteous people to possess the promised land, but, as long as its occupants are faithful, they will prosper. Eventually, the Nephites will be unfaithful enough and will be destroyed, but the Lamanites will not. If these are the tenets that Jarom's people—or at least the leaders—take as gospel, then they would understand any Nephite deviation from righteousness to be a literal threat to their lives. For Jarom and his contemporaries, the stakes of their fathers' prophecies translate into care for this singular, covenant land. Accordingly, both Enos and Jarom tell how the people use the land and its resources. Enos writes that his people cultivated the land, producing grain, fruit, cattle, goats, and horses (Enos 1:21). Jarom describes their wealth and industry; how they fortified their cities; acquired precious metals; and constructed buildings, machinery, tools, and weapons. But because prophecies about the covenant equate faithfulness with continuing to occupy the land and prosper thereon, the Nephites may be prone to equate economic plenty and growth with validation of their righteousness. Thus, Enos and Jarom's description of Nephite industriousness and wealth might also be read as a claim to righteousness evidenced by prosperity.

Finally, and perhaps most notably, it is possible to interpret the revelations of the Lehite founding fathers in such a way that Lamanite wickedness, relative to the Nephites, fulfills or corroborates the prophecies. If the prophecy says that the Lamanites will dwindle in unbelief, then any evidence of their dwindling can be taken as a point on the Nephite worldview scorecard. That is, Nephites could see Lamanite waywardness as confirming the prophecies and as evidence of their own righteousness and superiority. In this interpretation, the prophecies incentivize the Nephites to think ill of the Lamanites. Of course, Nephi, Jacob, and Enos's prophetic visions attest the reality and consequence of Lamanite iniquity. But it is easy to see how, with hard feelings already existing between the two groups, viewing Lamanite sins as confirmation of God's revelation or even as God's will, could increase Nephite prejudices against the Lamanites.

So we have a situation in which the path to distrusting and maybe even hating the Lamanites is made a little smoother. More troublingly, some may opt for that path under the guise of faith in Nephite prophecy. To be fair to the Nephites, it is hard to know what to do, how to think, or how to feel toward the Lamanites within the context of the Lehite founders' visions. Jesus said love everyone (treat them kindly, too). But Jesus also

said that the Lamanites would destroy the Nephites. If you're a Nephite, how do you smile that frown away?

the book of Jarom for our day

It is important to consider the Nephite perspective on Lamanites and prophecies because as church members we so often automatically relate to or identify with the Nephites. My general experience being raised in The Church of Jesus Christ of Latter-day Saints has been, at least in North America, that we champion the Book of Mormon as specifically American scripture written for our day. In our enthusiasm for what it offers, we take lessons from its pages and apply them to our ideas about the European settlement of the Americas and the founding of the United States; about forms of government and patriotism; about modern secret combinations, church organization, and many other aspects of our contemporary life. In all this application, we typically draw parallels between ourselves, as members of the church, and the members of the church who are the most visible in The Book of Mormon. That is, we liken ourselves to the Nephites. Serious students of the Book of Mormon have benefitted in countless ways from such comparison. We seek to emulate Nephi's obedience or Captain Moroni's steadfastness. We recognize how spreading power among a democratic system of judges avoids certain political risks posed by a monarchy. We aspire to faith unto deliverance like the peoples of Limhi or Alma₁.

If, however, we follow the comparison between modern members of the church and Nephites to its end, the picture is sobering. What does it mean if we identify with the Nephites, and the Nephites are destroyed? It means that we, like the Nephites, are susceptible and even inclined to sin, violence, and war. It means that we, like the Nephites, are almost guaranteed to be too comfortable with subtle forms of racism, sexism, and corruption. Seeing ourselves as like the Nephites should destroy our self-satisfaction with our own faithfulness. It should alert us that, as a people, we probably don't notice when we are falling into pride.[7] It should nudge us to recognize that others, even those we may regard as enemies, may, in the end, be more righteous and more qualified to occupy the land than we are. It should decenter the Gentiles from the picture and the purpose of the Book of Mormon; they play a critical role, to be sure, but this book is written first and foremost "to the Lamanites, who are a remnant of the house of Israel; and, [secondarily], also to Jew and Gentile" (title page). One of the main messages of these early revelations to Nephi, Jacob, and Enos is that the Book of Mormon is the means of salvation for Lehite descendants. Those descendants are the book's principal reason for existing.

With these warnings inherent to the Book of Mormon in mind, we should rethink what it means to identify with the Nephites, specifically in Jarom's account, including their attitudes toward the Lamanites. As already pointed out, a certain interpretation of Nephite prophecy tends to motivate the Nephites to a more negative view of the Lamanites, and anything the Lamanites do to reinforce that view could feel like a victory for the Nephites. It isn't difficult to transfer such attitudes to our own situation. If we strive to be not of the world, then others who exhibit what we think of as worldly interests, choices, language, or habits solidify our sense of security through our differences. Some take a kind of satisfaction or even pleasure in observing what they deem to be worldliness or wickedness in others since, to them, it confirms their religious views. They see troubles—fatherless families, teen pregnancies, convicted criminals, drug addicts, and so on—and their hearts fail them: they see signs of the times rather than children of God in need. Like the Nephites, all too often we judge others and look forward more to the prophesied apocalypse than to helping. It is so easy to respond this way while feeling confident in our status as chosen.

Theologians have a term for this orientation toward an oncoming destruction that is followed by some form of utopia: *millenarianism*. ☞ It isn't necessary for our purposes here to insist on the technical term, but it's worth knowing that Jarom's Nephites and our modern church aren't the only groups to have thought about it.

☞ In some cases *millenarianism* refers to any belief in a coming millennium of peace and prosperity, but most often theologians distinguish millenarianism's focus on the catastrophes that come before the millennium from *millennialism's* focus on a peaceful transition from the present state to the utopian state.

Put simply, millenarianism anticipates the end of days or some kind of decimating catastrophe, and it expects that things must get really bad to usher in the awaited cataclysmic change. It combines terror and hope—terror at what must happen before the fulfillment of all hopes is possible.

It's understandable how people come to adopt a millenarian perspective. Our scriptures abound with signs of Christ's second coming, many of which do not sound encouraging: "The sun shall be turned into darkness, and the moon into blood" (Acts 2:20, see also Rev. 6:12). "A time of trouble, such as never was..." (Dan. 12:1). "The love of men shall wax cold, and iniquity shall abound" (D&C 45:27). There will be "wars and rumours of wars" and "famines, and pestilences, and earthquakes" and these are only "the beginning of sorrows" (Matt. 24:6–8). No wonder that "fear shall come upon all people" (D&C 88:91).[8] All these frightening events precede Christ's return. The difficulty with focusing on these signs is that they can breed fear more readily than faith. Nevertheless, the scriptures *also* abound with opportunities to anticipate the Savior's coming with hope. The "gospel of the kingdom shall be preached in all the world" (Matt. 24:14) and a "light shall break forth among them that sit in darkness, and it shall be the fulness of my gospel" (D&C 45:28). Zenos's allegory of the olive tree describes the time before the second coming of Christ as the era when "branches began to grow and thrive exceedingly" (Jacob 5:73). Modern revelation assures that "the Lamanites shall blossom as the rose" (D&C 49:24). And so on.

It's important to remember that both kinds of signs are, in fact, prophetic. Whether we embrace the comforting images while denying the negative ones or obsess over the scary parts while downplaying the affirming events, we are wresting scripture by "cherry-picking" either way. With such an approach we find only what we have already decided to see instead of being sincerely open to what the scriptures can teach us. So, acknowledging that both kinds of prophecies are there, we must judge wisely. If the question is simply whether we recognize the signs, we can turn on the news and wring our hands until we inevitably throw them up in despair. Just look at this world, going to the telestial kingdom in a handbasket! But we can also look around and consider what we need to do to prepare for the second coming. In a nutshell, we can contrast these two modes of looking forward to the Savior's coming by asking, "Does the world need to get bad enough, or do the Lord's covenant people need to become good enough for Jesus to come again?" This divides the signs into those that require that we act and those in which we are acted upon. If some things, like natural disasters, widespread hunger, and horrific wars will happen, we can and should watch for and notice them. But other signs depend on the discipleship of God's covenant people to bring them about. If we do not roll up our sleeves and dig in, we give up our opportunity to share hope and redemption. We give up our place among the covenant people. The perspective we take will make all the difference in how we understand our responsibilities and responses to signs of the latter days.

the messianic

Nephi, Jacob, and Enos foresee a record from the Nephites saving the Lamanites in some future day and future Lamanites, in turn, saving the Lehite branch by restoring it to the house of Israel. All of that is far in the future from the perspective of the itty bitty books, which are centuries before even the first coming of Christ. Likewise, the origin story of the Lehites—their genesis as a people, their arrival in a holy, promised land, and their identity as a covenant people of God— is, for Enos, Jarom, Omni, and company, centuries in the past. The plates have been passed to successive generations, and these custodians of the record find themselves squarely in the middle of the dispensation, not during any particularly exciting time, at least from a religious-history perspective. What does it look like to live and keep faith in the middle of a dispensation? The book of Jarom is particularly instructive in this regard.

The anxiety surrounding Nephite righteousness and Lamanite iniquity in these post-Nephi small plates offers a model for our time as we anticipate our own end of days. We might assume that our situation is different from theirs because our next major event is the second coming of the Lord. In contrast, those Nephites really had nothing to worry about because all the prophecies indicated that they would not be destroyed until after the Savior had visited their land. Before that critical ingredient in the timeline, the Nephites could sit pretty. But Jarom tells us that the prophets, priests, and teachers of his generation didn't see it that way. Instead, they taught the people to "look forward unto the Messiah, and believe in him to come *as though he already was*" (Jarom 1:11, emphasis added). This changes everything.

What does it mean to look forward and believe in something to come as though it already was? Nephi describes what this looks like. He acknowledges that disciples of Christ who have entered the gate of baptism and are on the path to eternal life could not have "come thus far save it were by the word of Christ with unshaken faith in him, relying wholly upon the merits of him who is mighty to save" (2 Ne. 31:19). These disciples rely wholly upon the merits of him who, in Nephi's time, had not yet come. Even so, Nephi affirms that it is still possible to "press forward with a steadfastness in

Christ, having a perfect brightness of hope, and a love of God and of all men" (2 Ne. 31:20). Together, these statements show us a God who operates outside of human time. He and his atonement can stretch back to those who preceded him on earth and also reach forward into our future destiny.

With this in mind, if we return to the question of what it means to look forward to and believe in Christ as though he already was, we can think of it like a superpower. This kind of relationship with Christ indicates a freedom from linear time, shrugging off the obligation to live everything as if it unfolded on a simple, one-dimensional line. If we anticipate Christ this way, we're free from the temporal confines in which everything that came before must influence what comes next, and where we can only act in one direction, reaching toward the future. We can have Christ in our lives now even though, on a calendar, we are between his comings to earth. We can find Christ not just at the beginning and the end but also in the middle.

Even when we have this kind of relationship with Christ, we still use calendars. It isn't as though time no longer exists. So how does this work? Paul wrote to the Corinthians about how we can have a relationship with something that is and is not as it seems. He said, "the time is short: it remaineth, that both they that have wives be as though they had none; And they that weep, as though they wept not; and they that rejoice, as though they rejoiced not; and they that buy, as though they possessed not" (1 Cor. 7:29–30). This is the *as not* passage. It can seem here that Paul simply isn't making sense, or at least that he is contradicting himself. But he marks a pattern that is familiar to any Christian. Isn't Jesus's death, in a way, as though he died not? Isn't the law satisfied as though it wasn't broken? When we are forgiven, although our sins were as scarlet, aren't they made white as snow? It's no coincidence that all of these examples are related to Christ. In theological conversations, this way of relating to things is known as the *messianic*. In gospel discussions we frequently use the word *messianic* to describe anything relating to Christ as a deliverer and, in particular, to prophecies of his coming. In the field of Christian theology, however, while this usage works perfectly well, theologians sometimes use the term more narrowly to describe a suspended time and space that opens up for something new. The messianic isn't subject to the constant drum of time and the constraints of inhabiting space, as we tend to experience them in mortality. It's the *as not* way of being. It's a time and space where we actually have hope of overcoming the world even though we, ourselves, can never fulfill the demands of the law or vanquish death. It's when Christ intervenes and turns things inside out—when he turns the bad, the insuperable, and the damning to be as though they were not.

It is this messianic relationship to time and our own frailty that the leaders in Jarom's day were teaching the Nephites when they urged them "to look forward unto the Messiah, and believe in him to come," not as some distant event in the future, but "as though he already was" (Jarom 1:11). They adopted a different way of relating to Jesus, one that is already and always "in the now." As a result, they welcomed miracles and communion with God into their way of living. Although Jarom worries over the stiffneckedness and hard-heartedness of his people, he also confirms that "there are many among us who have many revelations, for they are not all stiffnecked. And as many as are not stiffnecked and have faith, have communion with the Holy Spirit" (Jarom 1:4). Even while the righteous leaders feared their own local apocalypse via Lamanite armies, many Nephites had many revelations and communed with the Holy Spirit.

Jarom makes it sound as though this kind of communion occurred regularly, as part of a common spiritual diet. He is almost casual about the abundance and constancy of his own spirituality that must be subordinated to the size constraints of the small plates: "wherefore, it must needs be that I write a little; but I shall not write the things of my prophesying, nor of my revelations. For what could I write more than my fathers have written? For have they not revealed the plan of salvation? I say unto you, Yea; and this sufficeth me" (Jarom 1:2). Jarom has prophecies and revelations, and, if we read between the lines, prophecies and revelations that are similar to those of his fathers. We have already seen the magnitude and import of Lehi, Nephi, Jacob, and Enos's prophecies. If Jarom is metaphorically batting with them, he, too, is in the spiritual big leagues.[9] Jarom, however, does not feel that his ministry requires that he disclose the scope or impressiveness of his revelations. The necessary prophecies have already been recorded, and, he tells us, "this sufficeth me." Instead, Jarom maintains the plates for the purpose accorded them in the prophecies of his fathers. He makes this purpose explicit: "these things are written for the intent of the benefit of our brethren the Lamanites" (Jarom 1:2). In the face of limited space on the plates, Jarom deemphasizes his own spiritual experiences. If this pattern sounds familiar it's because we saw something similar in Enos.

To prioritize keeping a record that will benefit the Lamanites, Jarom minimizes our view of his spirituality. In other words, he empties himself in the service of the Lamanite descendants. This is *kenosis* again. And as we have already seen, Jarom is not the only one in his time who empties himself this way. Many others also keep an eye toward prophesied events instead of a limited and myopic view of their current situation only. Jarom refers to multiple prophets, priests, teachers, kings, and leaders who were "mighty men of faith," and to the many who had "many revelations" and "communion with the Holy Spirit" (Jarom 1:4, 7, 10–11). They were part of a community of spiritually-minded, covenant Nephites. They were those earnest in their service to both their Nephite contemporaries and to facilitating the path to the covenant for the Lamanites' latter-day posterity.

And yet a robust community of faithful Nephites is not how we often think of Jarom and his contemporaries. Growing up in the church I remember fellow Latter-day saints inferring that these small books, especially the books of Jarom and Omni, indicate how the Nephites had slipped spiritually. We may presume that because they wrote "a little," that they held the plates and spiritual matters in lower regard than their forebears did (Jarom 1:2). A closer look at what the book of Jarom (and of Omni) relates, however, shows that on the whole, they maintained covenants, prophecies, revelation, keeping the commandments, and communion with the Holy Ghost as high priorities, both individually and in communities. The authors and societies behind these small books may seem to be not as spiritual, dominant, or inspiring as other authors of the small plates, but we could look at them another way. The description of Jesus's self-emptying as found in the King James Version of the New Testament could be applied to these writers and their contemporaries: they "made [themselves] of no reputation" (Philip. 2:7). We should probably give the authors of the Jarom and Omni books more credit.

The writers of these small books kept their focus on the greater need for the plates rather than on themselves, and they managed to do so for a long time. Perhaps this is one example of what communal *kenosis* or self-emptying looks like. If Enos's account sets up the question of whether such collective self-emptying is possible, his own posterity supplies an affirmative answer over the next several generations as they diligently preserve the small plates.

the latter days, the messianic, and the messy middle

By now we've seen how the Nephites in Jarom's day take the prophecies of their ancestors seriously. These revelations are their guide to avoid destruction, so the leaders and teachers stay busy reminding the people that righteousness is essential. The Nephites also understand these small plates to be expressly for gathering the Lamanites in the latter days. They relate to Christ and his coming as though he has already come, placing themselves in an everlasting and ever-present state of redemption. We also have seen that if we, as members of the restored church in the twenty-first century, liken ourselves to the Nephites, we are likening to the group that was destroyed for its wickedness. Jarom's people exercised constant vigilance in keeping their covenants for fear of their own apocalyptic destruction. Like them, we, too, look forward to the coming of the Savior, but we await his second coming and are alert to its signs, including the signs of the end of times.

But if we, taking a cue from the prophets, priests, and teachers of Jarom's day, "look forward unto the Messiah and believe in him to come" the *second* time "as though he already was," what changes? Do we treat those around us differently if we act as though Christ is already here and reigning on the earth? Are we more attentive to building his kingdom? Do we take better care of the earth, knowing that it will be the Lord's home for (at least) the next thousand years? Such a perspective might change how we view the signs of the latter-days, shifting our attention from the threats to the responsibilities. In particular, it shifts our attention to the responsibilities of a relationship with the Messiah. The messianic, that is, looking to Christ as though he was already come, plays neither defensively nor offensively; it is simply living in Christ. It holds open a time and space for things to be right, to be changed, to be what they are but not as they are. In short, to be saved.

Some may protest, however, that Jarom and his people were mistaken about the timing of Christ's coming. From our vantage point now we can see that Jarom and his people weren't at the end of their dispensation. It turns out that they were deep in the middle. They looked forward and lived as though the Messiah to come already was, and yet it was centuries before he arrived. Are we in a similar position? Are we smack in the middle of the latter days? We know that our current dispensation will usher in the second coming of the Lord, but a dispensation can last a very long time and no one knows the hour (see Matt. 24:36)—or the year, or the decade, or the century that he will come. In general, scripture attends most closely to beginnings and endings, to the kind of events found in Genesis and in Revelation. But what about the middle? How do we live out the covenant between such defining moments?

Here is where these small books can help us. Rather than seeing them as a lag or slowdown in the narrative of spirituality among Lehi and Sariah's descendants, perhaps we have more in common with them than we realize. It has now been over a century since a revelation was received that was added to the Doctrine and Covenants.[10] Would we say of our day, however, that revelation has ceased? Of course not. In many ways it feels as though revelation continues to increase within the church. But if people 2,500 years from now were to look back, with one narrow selection of records from which to draw their conclusions, would it look as though revelation was booming in the early twenty-first century? Perhaps not.

We are no longer quite at the beginning of a dispensation. The church is established in many locations throughout the world. Membership has grown, and the church has spread, centralized, and institutionalized in ways that were impossible in the nineteenth century. Are we at the end of the dispensation, then? It is easier to describe a total picture of history with the benefit of hindsight, but we cannot use hindsight on our current moment. Perhaps the end will come very quickly, but there also seems to be much work left to do. Elder D. Todd Christofferson recently taught, "First, and crucial for the Lord's return, is the presence on the earth of a people prepared to receive Him at His coming."[11] Are we ready yet? If not, we are probably in the middle.

If we want models for how to live in the middle of this dispensation, we can look to other middles, like those of the small books. Remember the messiness of communal *kenosis* discussed in the previous chapter. How do we live in the messy middle, where we can't see how prophecies will be fulfilled or know who will end up playing for which side? One thing we've already found in Jarom is an emphasis on evaluating the worldviews we inherit. As we've seen, Jarom inherits both prophecies and prejudices from his father. Sifting through his inheritance, Jarom wisely sorts between what he holds onto and what he lets go. This example of wisdom and discipline typifies what the messy middle requires. When we find ourselves in the middle, the novelty, enthusiasm, and energy of an exciting beginning have largely worn off. But if it is not the end either, there isn't the culminating rush that comes from seeing the light at the end of the tunnel. In the metaphoric Great Plains of the pioneers' trek west, it can seem that all there is to do is walk and walk and walk and walk. While in the middle, many points of reference recede into invisibility. When we walk in the vast middle, are we even getting anywhere? Walking hundreds of miles can be drudgery, and day after day it looks as though the reward for our trouble is only more walking. Disoriented and tired, we surely need wisdom and discipline. But Jarom does not exemplify wisdom and discipline because he must get through the middle without seeing his way. On the contrary, the wisdom and discipline come because he sees.

Jarom's account shows people who see in a messianic way and those who do not. Weary in the middle, some of the people of Jarom's time need constant coaxing into righteousness "because of the hardness of their hearts, and the deafness of their ears, and the blindness of their minds, and the stiffness of their necks" (Jarom 1:3). Jarom writes that many others, however, "have many revelations, for they are not all stiffnecked" (Jarom 1:4). Some need threats from the prophets (Jarom 1:10), and others manage to endure well, "labor[ing] diligently, exhorting with all long-suffering..., persuading them to look forward unto the Messiah" (Jarom 1:11). The people of both approaches live in the middle of their dispensation. What makes the difference for those who found the strength, wisdom, and discipline to live it well? The difference is in how they see. Those with strength can see themselves *as not* in the middle but see or "look forward unto the Messiah, and believe in him to come as though he already was" (Jarom 1:11). Strength in the middle comes from the Messiah. He turns the slog of the middle into the freedom of the messianic.

In the messianic, the grind of the messy middle becomes *as not* a grind. In our relationship with the Messiah, like Jarom, we let go of that which simply isn't needed. We find the peace to leave out some things, to let them become invisible. Perhaps we do not need so desperately to see our progress, to confirm our expectations of prophecy, especially where those expectations may lead us to expect the worst in others. We can, in general, refrain—another usually invisible form of discipleship. Jarom tells what the people did not do: they "profaned not; neither did they blaspheme" (Jarom 1:5). Holding back certain responses or actions is usually thankless, a generally unrecognized form of fidelity and kindness. But Jarom's omissions improved the inheritance of the covenant. When we see the Messiah as though he already was, he sees us too. "When that which is perfect is come, then that which is in part [is] done away" (1 Cor. 13:10). Known as we are known, we don't have to clamor for validation. We see clearly in the peace of the messianic, and we refrain.

Besides leaving out some things, in the messianic we also gain the strength to maintain. In particular, we gain the strength to maintain and remain in the covenant. Two generations and two hundred years removed from the family that originated the covenant, it would be easy or even predictable that Jarom would let the inheritance of the plates and the covenant lag. The middle can be precarious in its relative invisibility. But, instead, Jarom makes explicit the intent that the plates benefit the Lamanites. He remains committed to the vision of what the plates will accomplish and how much depends on the Lamanites. In spite of the wars between the two peoples, he calls them "our brethren," foregrounding their kinship (Jarom 1:2). While Jarom is willing to have his account retreat into the background, he foregrounds the Lamanites and their posterity: "And as these plates are small, and as these things are written for the intent of the benefit of our brethren the Lamanites, wherefore, it must needs be that I write a little; but I shall not write the things of my prophesying, nor of my revelations. For what could I write more than my fathers have written?" (Jarom 1:2). What Jarom elects to maintain, namely, the purpose of the plates and their role in the covenant, shapes what he chooses to let go—his own reputation and others' attention to his spirituality. Jarom suggests that living in the messy middle means holding fast to covenants and holding lightly to judgments, prejudices, and conclusions that are not guaranteed to stand the test of time. Jarom teaches us how to refrain and let go, how to maintain and remain in the covenant. He shows us how to live in the messy middle by living in the messianic.

3

Omni

The book of Omni has more authors than any other book in the Book of Mormon. The text moves through them quickly, but without each of their contributions to the record, we may not have ended up with the small plates. The writers are Omni, Amaron, Chemish, Abinadom, and Amaleki, and the sizes of their contributions range from Chemish's sixty-nine words (in English) to Amaleki's 919 (more than the entire book of Jarom). The book of Omni is the last book in the small plates— plates which had been kept separate from the political and historical records. When Amaleki makes his last entry and then gives the small plates to King Benjamin, it closes a loop, bringing the small plates back together with the historical records. The book of Omni, however, takes a historical turn itself. It covers about 150 years and recounts several wars, the destruction of the "more wicked part of the Nephites" (Omni 1:5), the relocation of some Nephites under Mosiah's leadership and their alliance with the people of Zarahemla, the discovery of a record of the Jaredites, the expulsion of the Lamanites from the land of Zarahemla, and two Nephite expeditions to repossess the land of their inheritance.

Given this variety of topics, it is especially handy to start with a map of where we are headed in this book. With the possible exception of Amaleki, biographical details about the writers in Omni are thinner on the ground than anywhere else in the Book of Mormon. Still, by thinking through the historical context and continuing to pay attention to a writer's inheritance, we can unearth a bit about each one. With this background, we will then explore how the small plates' use of the word "contention" distinguishes between family relationships and civic and national communities. Moving from the familial to the national, we consider the implications of that shift across generations. Omni's curious emphasis on keeping genealogy helps us understand all of this. In short, genealogy, as we find it in Omni, reveals the family networks that preserve the Book of Mormon and organize God's covenant people.

All of this focus on the covenant can feel abstract and distant. It seems clear enough that the covenant is about families—but on a gigantic, numerous-as-the-sands-of-the-sea kind of scale. At such proportions, it can be difficult to sense how the covenant relates to us individually. We may even wonder how our identity as Christians maps onto the small plates' constant emphasis on the family. In the last part of the chapter we will follow the book of Omni as it circles back around to our closest family relationships and gives us the opportunity to ask and begin to answer, "What do families have to do with Jesus?"

The Book of Mormon ushered in the restoration of the fullness of the gospel, signaling that the long-prophesied covenant it contained was beginning to be fulfilled (see 3 Ne. 21:1–7). This volume of scripture is the signature text of this church that claims Jesus Christ as its head and eternal families as one of its signature teachings. These two theological foundations—devotion to Christ and sealed networks of families—intersect in the book of Omni, the last book entry in dictation order.[1] This final statement in what would be translated into the Book of Mormon invites us to ponder the relationship between our commitment to Christ and our commitment to families, an apt question for saints in the latter days and for the covenant overall.

book of Omni authors

OMNI

By the time of Omni, the designation "Nephite" seems to be a political and cultural descriptor rather than a spiritual one. Omni's grandfather, Enos, tried to restore Lamanites to the Nephites' faith, and Omni's father, Jarom, showed that the Lamanites did not keep the Law of Moses as the Nephites did. Omni himself, though, reports immediately that he "fought much" for "[his] people, the Nephites," to protect them from "their enemies, the Lamanites" (Omni 1:2). In the face of recurring violence, whatever restraint or objectivity Jarom showed toward the Lamanites seems to have degenerated into calcified political factions by Omni's time. For Omni, the idea that Lamanites are enemies no longer needs to be explained; it simply is. Only after reporting the violence, and perhaps as a comment of less importance, Omni confesses, "I of myself am a wicked man, and I have not kept the statutes and the commandments of the Lord as I ought to have done" (Omni 1:2). We should remember, however, that Omni inherits the plates from his father Jarom, who, as we've seen, was dedicated and steadfast in following the prophecies and commandments of his forebears. Perhaps Omni is just reporting that he did not live up to his father's standard. He was, at least, faithful enough to keep the plates and may have taught what they contain to his son, Amaron, who cites a teaching from an earlier account on the small plates. We can perhaps even see a hint of Omni's dedication in that he engraves on the plates at two different times, six years apart, giving the date both times (Omni 1:3). Enos and Jarom don't give dates until the end of their narratives, so if Omni was following the same pattern, he may have expected to hand off the plates after the first entry. As one commentator has conjectured, perhaps this battle-wise warrior thought he was about to die and made his first entry to ensure that he did his duty, but then he survived long enough to make another entry before transferring the plates to his son Amaron.[2]

AMARON

At first glance, Amaron seems to be a more straightforward choice than Omni to be the author of a sacred text. He writes more than his father before him or his brother after, and he writes about a prophecy. Amaron tells us he is among those Nephites who survived when the "the more wicked part of the Nephites were destroyed" (Omni 1:5). Curiously, he does not specify that the Lamanites killed them, only that "the Lord did visit them in great judgment" and that the righteous were spared from "their enemies," leaving open the possibility that there was a civil war of some sort (Omni 1:7). Further, Amaron attributes the destruction to fulfillment of a different wording of the covenant: "the Lord would not suffer...that the words should not be verified, which he spake unto our fathers, saying that: Inasmuch as ye will not keep my commandments ye shall not prosper in the land" (Omni 1:6). In all this, Amaron looks like an upright guy. He outlives the events that killed the wicked Nephites, adds more than a cursory entry on the plates, and quotes scripture to boot.

Are things so clear, though? Amaron understands the Nephites' ruin to be the Lord verifying his word, and yet, as Grant Hardy has observed, we have no record of the words Amaron quotes.[3] Lehi reports the promise as, "Inasmuch as ye shall keep my commandments ye shall prosper in the land," with the consequence for failure being that "ye shall be cut off from my presence" (2 Ne. 1:20). Amaron's similar but inverted quotation—"inasmuch as ye will *not* keep my commandments ye shall *not* prosper" (emphasis added)—seems to portray a vengeful god who is more concerned with punishing the wicked than blessing the righteous. It's like an inverted prosperity gospel that labels the wicked by the calamities they suffer. Perhaps Amaron simply believes that eventually the wicked will get their comeuppance, or maybe he was just hurrying to finish and give the plates to Chemish.

CHEMISH

It isn't clear why Amaron gave the plates to his brother, Chemish, or why Omni didn't give the plates to Chemish instead of Amaron in the first place. We could speculate why—Amaron did not have a son (and could not imagine passing the record to a daughter), or he thought his child would not preserve the record. Or perhaps Omni thought Amaron was more spiritual, more mature, or more talkative than the laconic Chemish, and so on—but the text doesn't say. Whatever the reason, the plates made their way to Chemish, and he wrote a few lines that point to an incipient procedure for passing them on. This procedure warrants some notice.

Chemish reports that he saw Amaron write his last entry on the same day the plates were transferred—"and after this manner we keep the records"

(Omni 1:9). Does "after this manner" suggest that, by this point, the process of passing the records had become formalized? Later, in Alma 37, we find a solemn and lengthy process for conferring the plates and their accompanying sacred artifacts, but the exchange between Amaron and Chemish appears to have been much simpler. Despite this simplicity and even in his terseness, Chemish acknowledges his duty "according to the commandments of our fathers," using the same idea of a "command" or "commandment" that Jacob, Jarom, Omni, and, later, Alma₂, use (Omni 1:9; Alma 37:1). Chemish may have been like his grandfather Jarom in that he preferred his life to be a sermon rather than his words. Respect for his fathers' heritage and commands regarding the plates seems to be at least part of Chemish's motivation for receiving and transferring the record. Like his brother, Chemish was among the righteous who were spared when the "more wicked part of the Nephites were destroyed" (Omni 1:5). Moreover, Chemish fathered a son who was open enough to revelation to flee with Mosiah to the land of Zarahemla.

ABINADOM

The plates continue from Chemish to his son, Abinadom, who, like his grandfather, Omni, writes of his involvement in wars with the Lamanites, affirming that he has killed many of them with his own sword. Abinadom is aware of other Nephite plates, identifying the record "had by the kings" as "the record of this people" (Omni 1:11). He knows the sacred purpose of the small plates and so refrains from writing at length because, like Jarom, he "know[s] of no revelation save that which has been written, neither prophecy" (Omni 1:11). This care on Abinadom's part suggests that he may have been more attuned to the records and their purposes than the preceding authors, and this perhaps because he was a steward of the small plates during an exodus. Because his son, Amaleki, "was born in the days of Mosiah," Abinadom seems to have been among those who heeded the "voice of the Lord" and fled with Mosiah out of the land of Nephi (Omni 1:12, 23). As custodian of the plates, Abinadom probably carried the small plates to Zarahemla. He also seems to have known the records well enough to state that all the revelations that needed to be written had been. And perhaps we can see his commitment to help the plates fulfill their prophesied role in his statement: "that which is sufficient is written" (Omni 1:11). He doesn't say that that which is written is sufficient, as though it would just have to be adequate. Instead, he seems to have assessed what would meet the requirements of the prophecies—what would be sufficient to the record's destiny—and that, he determined, had been written. Having thus satisfied himself, he made "an end" (Omni 1:11).

We'll discuss Abinadom's son, Amaleki, more below. In the meantime, piecing together the context, inheritance, and self-presentation of each writer in Omni reveals his individuality as well as some of the flux of family dynamics. Having seen these dynamics at a granular level in this family line, we can examine the differences between domestic families and bigger tribal and civic communities. One of the ways the Book of Mormon distinguishes these levels of sociality is in how it uses the word *contention*.

contention

Some form of the word *contention* occurs three times in the book of Omni, and the ways it shows up sketch what the word means in the Book of Mormon more broadly. We can see that contention has a lot to do with war. First, Abinadom reports "much war and contention" between the Nephites and the Lamanites (Omni 1:10). Amaleki relays that the Mulekites had had "many wars and serious contentions" (Omni 1:17). Amaleki also tells of "a contention," describing an event in which a stubborn leader caused fighting among his own followers such that most of them were killed (Omni 1:28). Here, the contention is not on the scale of a war, but the effects are similarly deadly. In all three cases, "contention" involves a severe breach between groups of people that includes lethal violence.

The collective malice and threat of physical harm that accompanies contention in these examples does not match the way I usually hear the word "contention" used in Church settings. We tend, it seems, to take our bearings from a more familiar verse on contention. In 3 Nephi 11:29, Jesus teaches: "he that hath the spirit of contention is not of me, but is of the devil." Many members of the church know this verse as one of twenty-five selected from the Book of Mormon in the days of seminary scripture mastery. Since 1967, seventeen general conference talks have quoted this verse, usually referring to contention as a problem between individual family members. As a result, when we think about contention, most of the time we think about how to avoid an unhappy dynamic within our homes. To loosely quote a well-loved film, perhaps we should ask ourselves, "We keep using that word. Do we know what that word means? I do not think it means what we think it means." And yet, the sermon in the Book of Mormon that most directly counsels against bad feelings among family members does not mention contention. King Benjamin lived through many wars and contentions (see W of M 1:12–18), but when he speaks of family harmony he teaches, "ye will not suffer your children that they... fight and quarrel one with another, and serve the devil" (Mosiah 4:14). He seems to reserve the word "contention" for contexts other than the domestic.

If we take Benjamin's instruction for families together with Christ's admonition against contention, we can see how the two are related but also how they differ. Both passages connect negative feelings to the devil, whether in the context of fighting and quarreling or in the context of contention. The degree of severity is not the same, however. According to Benjamin, fighting and quarreling with siblings can be part of serving the devil. But, as Jesus explains, someone who has the spirit of contention isn't just helping the devil but has escalated to being *of* the devil—of his ilk, on his team. This suggests that while fighting and quarreling should definitely be avoided, they are different in degree from contention.

What, then, is contention? The word appears eighty-four times in the Book of Mormon. Not once, in all of these citations, is it used to refer clearly to conflict between individuals. ☞ In every case it identifies a societal or community conflict. Contention usually happens at the political level and sometimes involves religious topics.[4] It frequently appears (at least twenty-five times) in conjunction with war, dissension, bloodshed, murder, and political intrigue. Consider some examples: Nephi specifies that his large plates are for "an account of...the wars and contentions of my people" (1 Ne. 9:4). Lehi teaches his sons that New-World and Old-World scriptures would "grow together, unto the confounding of false doctrines and laying down of contentions" (2 Ne. 3:12). Mosiah writes "that there should be no wars nor contentions, no stealing, nor

☞ The closest it comes to referring to such intimate relationships is when Alma the Elder, at the waters of Mormon, instructs his new converts "that there should be no contention one with another, but they should...[have] their hearts knit together in unity and in love one towards another" (Mosiah 18:21).

86

plundering, nor murdering, nor any manner of iniquity" (Mosiah 29:14). According to him, "ye cannot dethrone an iniquitous king save it be through much contention, and the shedding of much blood" (Mosiah 29:21). In all these texts, contention is more severe and physically violent than a family spat at dinner. Contention collectivizes and mobs, wishes and inflicts bodily harm, pits one people against another, and mobilizes hatred. *This* is contention as the Book of Mormon portrays it, and this is what's of the devil. ☛

Although smaller, intimate arguments are not what the Book of Mormon means by the word *contention,* if the Book of Mormon offers any kind of message to families, it is that this kind of familial strife still begs for our care and preventive attention. Benjamin's caution implies that family habits of fighting and quarreling can lead down the same path as the contention the Lord condemns. The founding family of the Book of Mormon begins with differences of opinion about Lehi's visions, the decision to go into the wilderness, how to obtain the brass plates, and so on. Such differences are normal within families. But Nephi and Laman are never able to really put these differences to rest, and their conflicts snowball into contentions on a national scale.

The only times that the word *contention* appears in Nephi's record is in prophecies of the future or when he explains that the people's contentions are recorded on the large plates.Jacob, however, elegizes that he and his people are "wanderers, cast out from Jerusalem, born

☛ I focus on the word *contention* for this study. The Book of Mormon also includes forty-one uses of the word *contend.* Contrary to the use of the word *contention,* the word *contend* occasionally denotes strife between individuals. Still, the word *contend* suggests that the contending individual approaches an interaction with a pre-determined decision to resist whatever the identified adversary does or will do. Note also that in a few cases the Lord declares that he will contend on behalf of his covenant people. Perhaps the spirit of contention is of the devil but contending may not always be so designated.

in tribulation, in a wilderness, and hated of our breth-ren, which caused wars and contentions; wherefore, we did mourn out our days" (Jacob 7:26). Enos reports that people had to be reminded of the likelihood and dan-ger of contention if they slacked off, but he does not cite contention as a regular challenge (see Enos 1:23). By Jarom's generation, though, contention is not a hov-ering threat but a recurring reality "much of the time" (Jarom 1:13). Finally, the book of Omni mentions con-tention more than any of the previous small books; it has, by then, become the way of things. What had only been potential in Nephi's record was the norm five gen-erations later with Abinadom. The first mention of con-tention between the Nephites and Lamanites in real time is Jacob's mournful summary when he says that the Nephites were "hated of [their] brethren" (Jacob 7:26). It may be a bridge too far to say that a run-of-the-mill disagreement with your in-law is "contention." If the disagreement isn't healed, though, it threatens to become the outsized inheritance of future generations who may well find themselves embroiled in "wars and contentions" with a people they do not even know but who are, nevertheless, their kin.

genealogy: are they doing it?

We have just seen how the threat of contention that hangs over societies and nations can get its start from our families' domestic relationships. Small and simple things, including the wrong small and simple things, can bring great and terrible things to pass. Quarrels within families can tear nations apart. But the book of Omni also shows how to stitch families and nations together across time. It begins with Omni's stated pur-pose for keeping the plates. Following his father's lead, Omni says he is to write on the plates "to preserve our genealogy" (Omni 1:1 and Jarom 1:1).

Nowhere in the Book of Mormon is the mechanism for preserving the plates (to say nothing of preserving genealogy) so visible as it is in Omni. We see the plates transferred through five writers in just eleven verses. And, at first glance, nowhere do Book of Mormon authors seem to lose sight of the reason for the plates like they do in the book of Omni. Beginning with Omni's announcement that he has been commanded to keep the plates to preserve genealogy, the succession of records detailed in the book of Omni seems at odds with the plates' purpose as Nephi outlined it. According to Nephi, the small plates are for the things of the spirit, for prophecies, and for purposes known to God (see 1 Ne. 9:3, 19:3, 5; 2 Ne. 5:29–30). Nephi explicitly says, however, that these plates are not to give the genealogy of his fathers:

> And now I, Nephi, do not give the genealogy of my fathers in this part of my record; neither at any time shall I give it after upon these plates which I am writing; for it is given in the record which has been kept by my father; wherefore, I do not write it in this work. (1 Ne. 6:1)

We must ask then if Jarom and Omni's turn toward genealogy is misguided. Have they altered the use and intent of the small plates?

Jarom seems to flout precedent when he says that he writes in order "that our genealogy may be kept" (Jarom 1:1). But, as we saw in the previous chapter, Jarom clearly understands the covenant. He shows how Nephite society was built around the expectation that the covenant would be fulfilled. If Jarom foregrounds genealogy, presumably it is because he understands it to be vital to the mission of the plates, and Omni follows suit. Moreover, Nephi explains that the genealogy of his fathers will never be found in the small plates, but that genealogy is different than the one that Jarom and Omni keep. Theirs is the record of Nephi's and, more precisely, Jacob's posterity, from Nephi, the first king of his people, to Benjamin, the penultimate king of the Nephite civilization before the reign of the judges. The genealogy they keep marks natural boundaries on either end of a distinct era in Book of Mormon history.

Furthermore, the genealogy kept in these smallest books of the small plates is less like a traditional genealogy in holy writ and more like a group journal. We know that what we might call "regular" genealogy was known to the Nephites, since Lehi scours the brass plates for his own genealogy. Later in the book of Omni, Mosiah and his people ask Zarahemla, the Mulekite leader, to give "a genealogy of his fathers, according to his memory," and then write it down (Omni 1:18). These are traditional modes of keeping genealogy in holy writ. What we find at the beginning of the book of Omni is clearly a different project. Are the writers in Omni really doing genealogy if they are looking forward instead of in retrospect? It is as though I wrote a few lines about my own life and called it genealogy. If I then give the record to my son with the responsibility to write and hand it down to his children, the end result may look something like genealogy. During my lifetime, though, it just looks like a journal.

Why, then, does genealogy become so important in these short books? Of many possible responses, here are a few: 1. The instruction to keep genealogy also keeps the plates circulating into future generations, connecting families and scripture. 2. The practice of genealogy represented in these plates keeps both oral and written prophetic traditions alive for the leaders of the Lehite faithful. 3. Structurally, the book of Omni (and the small plates as a whole) is shot through with the task and impact of genealogy and family relation-ships. It's worth our time to unpack each of these in turn.

the reasons why they are doing it

What does the genealogical turn here at the end of the small plates teach us theologically? First, the manner in which this genealogy is kept links kin and scripture and prevents both from being lost. Not all genealogies share the same form or purpose. Genealogies in Genesis 5:3–32 or Matthew 1:1–17 provide a series of "begats," a lineal list of who came from whom. Ether 1:6–32 offers a similar account in the Book of Mormon. In these small books, however, the genealogy is not spelled out after the fact by one author. Instead, it is preserved by keep-ing the plates moving from one set of hands to the next. Each author's entry, however brief, marks the contin-ued awareness of and commitment to these propheti-cally destined chronicles. It is like the story of the dying woman who requested that her surviving relatives take a family photo once a year. When questioned, she con-ceded that her real purpose was to make sure that the family got together at least once a year—the photo was incidental. In like manner, if each generation must write something to preserve the genealogy, one consequence is that the plates will be passed on and not be lost or left behind. The way to send a message to people centuries in the future is similar to the way to eat an elephant: one bite, or one generation, at a time.

In the small plates, the descendants of Jacob under-stand that each generation has a responsibility to write, no matter how minor the engraved contribution, and that no one can be a missing link. The caretakers of the plates verify, by their lifelong stewardship over the records, that the accounts are still what they claim to be and that they have remained with those who have an interest in their survival and integrity. King Benjamin explains this to his sons: "And behold, also the plates of Nephi...and they are true; and we can know of their surety *because we have them before our eyes*" (Mosiah 1:6, emphasis added). For Benjamin, the physical presence of the plates—with their self-declared chain of custody—certifies their truth. As the plates are handed down, keeping genealogy also means keeping the plates, so when the plates reach the next set of hands, preserved and intact, they maintain their integrity. The genealogy of this family becomes a genealogy of the plates themselves. It makes their origin and the path to their fulfillment in prophecy transparent, and each new generation reasserts and re-notarizes the legitimacy of that origin and that path. One function of the genealogy as Jarom and Omni announce it is thus to authenticate the record.

A second takeaway from these books' focus on genealogy is that it connects the small plates to other scriptural traditions. The small plates and their caretakers are deliberate about highlighting parallels between the small plates and the brass plates, particularly on the topic of genealogy. Lehi requests that his sons return to Jerusalem for the brass plates because "Laban hath the record of the Jews and also a genealogy of my forefathers" (1 Ne. 3:3). This language comes up in later transfers of the brass plates as well (see FIGURE 2 on following pages). Four generations after the end of the book of Omni, Alma the Younger gives all the plates in his possession to his son Helaman and charges him to keep a record of the people (Alma 37:1–2). This collection includes the plates of Nephi, the brass plates, the twenty-four plates of the Jaredite record, the interpreters or Urim and Thummim, and, it seems, the Liahona (Alma 37:2–3, 21, 24, 38).[5] Early in his instruction, Alma$_2$ says the brass plates "have the records of the holy scriptures upon them," or the "record of the Jews" as Lehi called it, and also "the genealogy of our forefathers, even from the beginning" (Alma 37:3). Alma$_2$ continues,

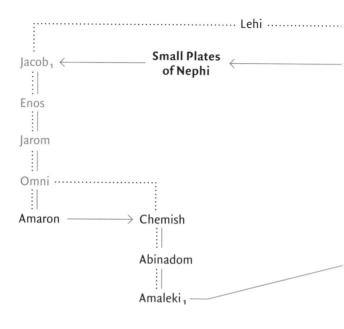

Lehi

Jacob₁ ← **Small Plates of Nephi** ←

Enos

Jarom

Omni

Amaron ⟶ Chemish

Abinadom

Amaleki₁

Genealogy	··········
Path of records	——
Record keepers with self-titled books	Mosiah₂

FIGURE 2

Record Keepers in the Book of Mormon

 Mormon₂, the figure for whom The Book of Mormon is named and its principal compiler, is referred to simply as Mormon throughout this book.

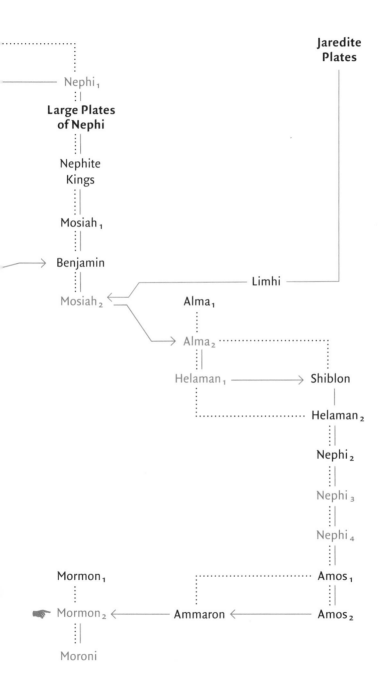

Jaredite
Plates

Nephi₁

Large Plates
of Nephi

Nephite
Kings

Mosiah₁

Benjamin

Mosiah₂   Limhi

Alma₁

Alma₂

Helaman₁ ⟶ Shiblon

Helaman₂

Nephi₂

Nephi₃

Nephi₄

Mormon₁   Amos₁

Mormon₂ ⟵ Ammaron ⟵ Amos₂

Moroni

> Behold, it has been prophesied by our fathers,
> that they should be kept and handed down
> from one generation to another, and be kept
> and preserved by the hand of the Lord until
> they should go forth unto every nation, kindred,
> tongue, and people, that they shall know of the
> mysteries contained thereon (Alma 37:4).

When Alma$_2$ instructs, "they should be kept," what records is he talking about? He has been discussing the brass plates, but the prophecies he quotes sound very much like those reiterated in each exchange of the small plates—they are handed down from one generation to another and destined to go forth to every nation, kindred, tongue, and people.[6] Also, distinct from the "forefathers" cited in the brass plates (1 Ne. 3:3, Alma 37:3), Alma$_2$ names these as prophecies of the Lehite "fathers" (Alma 37:4). In short, Alma$_2$'s language could apply to either set of records—the brass plates or the small plates. Did he get his wires crossed?

Perhaps the shared profile of the brass plates and the small plates here represents something larger. The indistinguishability of brass plates and small plates in this passage is an emblem for how scripture and genealogy combine in saving God's children. Of course the destinies of the brass plates and the small plates are not exactly the same. But up to this point, their paths and their continued trajectory to the latter days parallel the prophecies that they contain. The brass plates seem to be a remnant of a larger scriptural tradition in Israel, that is, the Kingdom of Israel, or ten tribes, distinct from the Kingdom of Judah. From Lehi's readings and teachings it is clear that the brass plates contain a genealogy of the tribe of Joseph (or of Ephraim and Manasseh) as well as extended prophecies about him. Most likely, these plates were brought from their land of

95

origin in the Northern Kingdom to Jerusalem when the northern kingdom fell to Assyria. Then, over Laban's dead body, the plates left Jerusalem, wandered in the wilderness for several years, and made their way across the ocean to the promised land.[7] The journey of the small plates is also far-reaching. Intended for latter-day descendants of Lehi and Sariah, the small plates arrive to their foretold readers not from the same geographical distance but from a greater temporal one. And, like the brass plates, the genealogy they contain teaches their readers who they are and their place among God's covenant people.

Throughout the Book of Mormon, several authors recite the transfer of plates, but nowhere more than in the book of Omni. Alma$_2$'s handoff to Helaman, however, spells out the process and instructions of the exchange at greater length than anywhere else. We can see how the tradition of passing down the plates develops over generations to the thorough tutelage that Alma$_2$ offers Helaman in Alma 37. And, listening for echoes of earlier exchanges, we realize that some of the traditions were established and refined well before this time.

Alma$_2$ opens with three specific directions for his son. The first two are a dual commandment: "I command you that ye take the records which have been entrusted with me; and I also command you that ye keep a record of this people, according as I have done, upon the plates of Nephi" (Alma 37:1–2). In this we hear echoes of Jacob (see Jacob 1:1–2; 7:27).[8] Alma$_2$ follows up with a third mandate: "and keep all these things sacred which I have kept, even as I have kept them; for it is for a wise purpose that they are kept" (Alma 37:2). Surely those who inherited the plates received some form of this third piece of instruction as well, to keep all these things sacred. It is clear that all the writers felt the importance of the plates and their responsibility to them. Even Chemish and Abinadom, who were more curt in their contributions, and Omni, who considered himself to be wicked, kept their responsibility to the plates in some form, if only through a short entry.

small and simple

By now we can see that the authors' contributions in these itty bitty books, however brief, accomplish a lot. These books, by highlighting the bestowal of the plates over and over, prepare us to better appreciate a teaching Alma$_2$ relates in transferring records to Helaman. While instructing him to keep these things sacred, Alma$_2$ gives an unexpected, pragmatic, and material detail: "if they are kept they must retain their brightness" (Alma 37:5). What does Alma$_2$ mean? Is this another way of saying that Helaman should not only keep the plates, but that he should spiritually value them also? When Lehi prophesied about the brass plates, he said they would go to all people, and that in so doing the brass plates would not be "dimmed any more by time" (1 Ne. 5:19). This is a kind of metaphoric way of thinking about the plates shining forth; as they go to all "nations, kindreds, tongues, and people who were of his seed," they aren't dimmed by time (1 Ne. 5:18). Lehi's prophecy is bold and far-reaching. Alma$_2$, though, seems to have something else in mind. He is not declaring a grand destiny for the record. On the contrary, he offers a near-apology and explains himself. After he tells Helaman that the plates must retain their brightness, he protests, "Now ye may suppose that this is foolishness in me; but behold I say unto you, that by small and simple things are great things brought to pass" (Alma 37:6). When Alma$_2$ says the plates must retain their brightness, he is talking about something small and simple. I think he is saying that the plates must be polished. 👉

Having just reiterated that both the small plates and brass plates will be preserved and go forth to all the world, is Alma$_2$ really interjecting with a mundane reminder to polish the plates? If we take his words literally, yes, he is. The plates aren't just to be stored but also to be kept, to be wiped clean and made smooth and shiny. Alma$_2$ seems to think that if the plates are cared for at the level of polishing and burnishing them—making sure that they retain their brightness—they will be adequately kept or preserved to fulfill the prophecies and covenants associated with them. Alma$_2$'s testimony of the power of the small and simple can be understood and applied in innumerable ways. But in its original context, Alma$_2$ is saying that even though polishing plates seems small, simple, and foolish, this tiny act will accomplish great things. To take Alma$_2$ literally surprises us. It sounds like a grandmother's fastidiousness over a beloved heirloom. How much good does regularly polishing the plates actually do? But that is the beauty of Alma$_2$'s example. He insists that really, truly, the thing that surely is too small and too tedious to pay much notice will, in the end, be the means of bringing great things to pass.

This is what the authors in the books of Enos, Jarom, and Omni are counting on. What better model of small things bringing great things to pass than reliably keeping genealogy from one generation to the next? Alma$_2$

☞ I use the familiar word *polish* loosely here as among the terms that archaeometallurgists apply to Mesoamerican metal artifacts. It is also worth noting that "the knowledge required for specialized [metallurgical] crafting was probably hereditary," and perhaps technical skills and knowledge for caring for metal was passed down this way as well. See Aaron N. Shugar and Scott E. Simmons, eds., *Archaeometallurgy in Mesoamerica: Current Approaches and New Perspectives* (Boulder: University Press of Colorado, 2013), 10 and 128. ProQuest Ebook Central. For additional information about metallurgy in ancient American contexts, see John L. Sorenson, *Mormon's Codex: An Ancient American Book* (Salt Lake City: Neal A. Maxwell Institute and Deseret Book, 2013), 331–44, especially 339–40.

and others clearly read from the small plates. In the 468 years between the time that Nephi first gave the plates to Jacob (542 BC) until Alma$_2$ taught Helaman about his duties (74 BC), it hardly seems likely that the plates would have remained readable without polishing and care. Some of the writers imply that there were practices attached to the commandment to keep the plates. In phrasing similar to Alma$_2$'s, Jarom closes his account by telling how he delivered the plates to his son, Omni, "that they may be kept *according to the commandments of my fathers*" (Jarom 1:15, emphasis mine; see also Omni 1:9). Perhaps at some point keeping the plates according to the commandments of the fathers entailed additional instructions to polish them or to make sure that they retained their brightness. When Benjamin recommends the plates to his sons, we can presume that the plates are legible since he says, "behold, also the plates of Nephi . . . we have them before our eyes. . . . I would that ye should remember to search them diligently" (Mosiah 1:6–7). Benjamin's exhortation provides a clue to Alma$_2$'s passion for brightness: if the plates are regularly polished, they are more likely to be read and less likely to be forgotten.

To come full circle, then, we have seen how the practice of recordkeeping that Jarom and Omni call genealogy preserves both plates and kinship lines. It connects the small plates to other sets of Book of Mormon records, and it also continues a rich literary trope around genealogy that links the book of Omni and the small plates to scriptural traditions as a whole. The book of Omni begins by explaining how Omni received the plates and preserved genealogy. It ends with the convergence of four sets of records: the small plates, the large plates, the twenty-four Jaredite plates, and the newly transcribed Mulekite oral history. Given how the Book of Mormon repeatedly associates scripture and genealogy, it seems likely that the Nephites and Mulekites viewed this transcribed account as a form of holy writ. Keeping genealogy doesn't just preserve scripture; it also creates it. In the final judgment, the books of life and of lives will be opened (Rev. 20:12). All the more reason to keep them now.

lineal and lateral links

As we've seen, these books show in rapid succession what each author inherits from the previous generation as well as what shape that inheritance takes in the succeeding generation. Let's review some of these hinge-points again to illustrate. Enos finds himself with serious biases toward the Lamanites, but he also secures a renewed assurance of their descendants' salvation. Jarom understands that his father's prophecies identify an enduring threat to Nephite survival, so he seeks to ensure that the Nephites won't be destroyed because of wickedness and also that their record will reach future Lamanites. Omni seems ashamed at not prioritizing faithfulness the way Jarom did and yet reiterates the obligation to preserve the genealogy while he continues to pass on the plates. Amaron recenters understanding the Nephites' survival or destruction in terms of their faithfulness or lack thereof; he reports that many Nephites were destroyed because they did not keep the commandments. We do not know why Amaron gave his brother Chemish the plates, but Chemish's willingness to receive them and maintain the practices of exchange, genealogy, and record-keeping proved pivotal to their survival. The chain swerved to a brother rather than a son, and the chain was not broken. Two generations later Amaleki also did not pass the plates to his child (because he had "no seed" [Omni 1:25]), and he placed the plates with someone he trusted to continue their care and longevity: King Benjamin.

From this quick recap, we see that two kinds of relationships coordinate the path of the plates. Much of the time the record passes from father to son, in lineal descent. Sometimes, however, instead of moving lineally, the plates transfer laterally, to a brother or peer. This pattern holds true throughout the Book of Mormon. (See FIGURE 2 on pages 93–94.)

There are twenty-two record transfers from Nephi down to Moroni. Fifteen of the transfers are lineal. The small plates have three lateral moves: Nephi to his brother Jacob, Amaron to his brother Chemish, and Amaleki to his king, Benjamin. From Benjamin the plates move lineally to Mosiah, but then they move laterally to Alma the Younger. Alma the Younger passes lineally to Helaman$_1$, who passes laterally to his brother, Shiblon, who then, to keep things interesting, passes laterally to Helaman's son, Helaman$_2$. The plates pass lineally for several generations until Amos, who passes laterally to his brother, Ammaron. (It is rather poetic to have Am[m]arons in fraternal exchanges flanking the early and late stages of the plates' circulation.) Ammaron passes laterally to Mormon, who passes lineally to Moroni.

These combinations of lineal and lateral handoffs account for the entire path of the plates from the time Nephi forged them until Joseph Smith carried them to his home. Like the miracles produced by small and simple things, as Alma$_2$ taught Helaman, the faithfulness of each individual caretaker of the plates cumulates in a miraculous delivery of the record across centuries, a metaphoric message in a bottle that washes up on shore at the other side of a temporal, linguistic, and cultural ocean. The preservation of genealogy, as the writers of the small plates understand it, make the route of the small plates a figure for the overall message of the Book of Mormon: we need continued, surviving relationships if we're going to make it. And when a relationship in one direction fails, a relationship of another kind can rescue what would otherwise be lost. When Nephi wishes to keep the sacred record separate from the monarchy, he gives the plates to his brother Jacob, the priest. When Amaleki does not have seed, he passes them to King Benjamin who does. Enos tells us that the Lamanites posed a serious threat to the plates; they sought to "destroy our records and us" (Enos 1:14). Sending the plates into the future where (when) they would eventually reach the Lamanites' lineal descendants thus became the way of saving both plates and Lamanites. From the future, the records would reach the Lamanites' seed, and their redemption would be the means of healing the fraternal rift that began in the Book of Mormon founding family. The final shift of the Nephite account into the hands of a future reader, a sister or brother from the latter-day remnant, completes the chain. When Lehite posterity hold the book today, no matter which line they come from, the record moves lineally and laterally once more.

The lateral links universalize the Book of Mormon's audience. Although the Lamanites are named multiple times in the Book of Mormon as the primary intended recipients of the record, in reality contemporary "Lamanites" descend from all the lines in the Book of Mormon's first family—and from many other ancestors too. Mormon noted that after an era of peace when there was no manner of -ites, the people began again to split into factions. They reverted to the multiple groupings originating from Lehi and Sariah's family and became the Nephites, Jacobites, Josephites, and Zoramites on the Nephite side and the Lamanites, Lemuelites, and Ishmaelites on the Lamanite side (Morm. 1:8–9). Although they reduced these groups to just Nephites and Lamanites, Nephi saw, even in the originary vision of the Book of Mormon's destiny, that the remnant who would receive this scripture in the latter days descended not exclusively from Laman and Lemuel (1 Ne. 13:34; 14:2). When he explained the prophecy to his brothers, Nephi referred to those who would be reclaimed by the house of Israel as "our seed," the posterity of both him *and* his brothers (1 Ne. 15:12–14).

Ultimately, the covenant of the Book of Mormon doesn't just redeem the Lamanites but all the family of Lehi and Sariah and all those who have joined them (see D&C 3:17–18). The crossover of lineal and lateral connections across time links all these networks, connecting those who transmit and those who read the record that becomes the Book of Mormon. Because the plates and their story move both ways, they capture all the associated individuals and families not only in a chain but in chain mail, surrounded by linkages lineally and laterally, stretching in all directions. The chain-mail links include those in less traditional family situations who may not fit neatly into a conventional lineal inheritance, such as those who never married, widows and widowers, LGBTQ+ people, those who cannot have children, those who die prematurely, families who are separated, and anyone who cannot care for others. God wants all to be included in the covenant family. As Joseph Smith explains, "And now, my dearly beloved brethren and sisters, let me assure you that these are principles in relation to the dead and the living that cannot be lightly passed over, as pertaining to our salvation. For their salvation is necessary and essential to our salvation, as Paul says concerning the fathers—that they without us cannot be made perfect—neither can we without our dead be made perfect" (D&C 128:15).

"what do families have to do with Jesus?"

At the end of the book of Omni, which, in dictation order, is the end of the entire Book of Mormon, books and families converge. The Nephites flee and join with the Mulekites, who, because they do not preserve their own records, are subsumed into the account of the Nephites. The Nephites and Mulekites learn of the Jaredites and find their record, experiencing in microcosm the destiny of the small plates that will reveal Lehi and Sariah's family to a future people. In these two encounters, the Nephites read and interpret records and renew their appreciation for language and the ability to translate. In particular, Amaleki rejoices in the gifts that make possible a communal embrace of other peoples, whether in person (the Mulekites) or through their records (the Jaredites). He exhorts all to "come unto God, the Holy One of Israel," recognizing the one being under whom Israel unites (Omni 1:25). And he urges readers to "believe in prophesying, and in revelations, and in the ministering of angels, and in the gift of speaking with tongues, and in the gift of interpreting languages, and in all things which are good" (Omni 1:25).

In Amaleki's account, speaking and interpreting, and tongues and language are part of coming to God and, particularly, coming to Christ: "And now, my beloved brethren, I would that ye should come unto Christ, who is the Holy One of Israel, and partake of his salvation, and the power of his redemption. Yea, come unto him...and as the Lord liveth ye will be saved" (Omni 1:26). Amaleki connects coming unto Christ with a series of spiritual gifts, especially those that allow us to communicate across languages, cultures, and time, via the written word. He finishes his first farewell with a promise that sounds quite Protestant: "ye will be saved." Often we draw fault lines that distinguish a Protestant heaven—being saved—from heaven as it is depicted in the restored Church, that is, enjoying eternal families.

But Amaleki's benediction evokes a sense of both kinds of heaven. Amaleki invites us to "partake" of salvation and redemption in the present tense.[9] He portrays salvation that is immanent—right here, right now, much like the prophets in Jarom's day taught the people to believe in the Messiah "as though he already was" (Omni 1:26 and Jarom 1:11). Amaleki also calls the Lord the Holy One of Israel. This is Israel's God, Israel with the widespread, covenantal family. In short, in Amaleki's invitation, we find the resonances of individual and communal salvation: "come unto Christ, who is the Holy One of Israel, and...ye will be saved." How distinct are these two senses of salvation? It may be that we try to keep them more separate than we need to.

I have heard some members of the Church express concern that in church conversations we focus so much on eternal families that we risk forgetting about Jesus. They ask: Are we the church of Jesus Christ or the church of eternal families?

In our church community, our conversations and discourse about families are imperfect and sometimes even insensitive to the variety of individual situations. Some families create more pain than joy. Still, the question is an important one, and it speaks to how far-ranging the church's aims are. These small books illustrate the immensity of both demands—that we become true Christians, saved by Jesus, and also champions of families and their potential to save. But it may be that the question of whether we are the church of Jesus Christ or the church of eternal families presumes a division between Jesus and families that isn't useful and that vastly underestimates Jesus's interest in and power to heal even the most broken of families, at least in eternity. Perhaps we should ask, "What do families have to do with Jesus? And what does Jesus have to do with families?" These questions press even when our families are awful and hurtful.

I recall a version of these two questions that I heard some years ago. Once, during a Sunday School discussion about eternal marriage, the class was considering what eternal families would look like. Comments ranged from the curious and quotidian: "Do we all go bowling together for a heavenly family activity?" to the concerning and cosmic: "Will we really not be able to see family members who did not receive the sealing covenant?" As we grappled with these questions, a wise class member observed, "Perhaps eternal families have little to do with domesticity."[10] His remark suggests that perhaps the anticipated reward of spending time with family, those we live with, grow with, and hopefully learn to love in this life, is not the primary priority or payoff of a temple sealing.

I have heard members of the Church suggest that heaven isn't so appealing if it consists merely of sitting on a cloud and playing a harp all day. This, of course, is an unfairly reductive portrayal of some Christian notions of salvation, but how much better is the idea of an endless family reunion? Perhaps this latter possibility is more appealing, but surely it, too, is inadequate to the crush of infinity, the unspooling of seconds, minutes, hours, days, weeks, months, years, decades, centuries, millennia, geologic eras, and cosmic eons in eternal life. To riff on family reunion traditions common to Utah, what exactly would we do once we had exhausted all the variations of talent shows, relay games, pie contests, and barbecues that we could think of? Sit on a cloud and play a harp for a little me-time? Perhaps eternal families have less to do with domesticity, indeed. The idea of the domestic gives short shrift to a human family on the scale of the Abrahamic covenant, numberless as the stars in the sky or sands of the sea.

And yet the directness with which the Book of Mormon speaks to your heart and mine, individually, on a particular day and in a specific way, bears all the trademarks of craftsmanship by one who knows us intimately.

These itty bitty books come to us that way, the final precision tip of the entire book, especially when read in
dictation order. Mormon himself tells us, his latter-day
readers, "Wherefore, I chose these things," these small
plates,

> to finish my record upon them, which remain-
> der of my record I shall take from the plates of
> Nephi; and I cannot write the hundredth part
> of the things of my people. But behold, I shall
> take these plates, which contain these prophe-
> syings and revelations, and put them with the
> remainder of my record, for they are choice
> unto me; and I know they will be choice unto
> my brethren (Words of Mormon 1:5–6).

Even before he had finished abridging the larger plates
of Nephi, Mormon decided that these small plates
would finish the record. Accordingly, he put them
at the end, making this book of Omni the end of the
entire Book of Mormon.

What, then, is the end of the book? Amaleki invites
all to come unto God, to believe in spiritual gifts
that gather families, and to offer their whole souls to
Christ. It is as heartfelt a closing as any among Book of
Mormon authors. In our mind's eye we can see Amaleki
conclude and put the stylus down, a satisfying ending.

Except that he is not satisfied.

He starts again, something on his mind,

> And now I would speak somewhat concerning
> a certain number who went up into the wil-
> derness to return to the land of Nephi.... And
> I, Amaleki, had a brother, who also went with
> them; and I have not since known concerning
> them. And I am about to lie down in my grave;

and these plates are full. And I make an end of
my speaking (Omni 1:27, 30).

[*end scene, curtain close*]

This is the end in dictation order. Amaleki presents us
with a beautiful rendition of the Christian message, but
even that isn't sufficient closure for his account. Why?
It's as though in his bones Amaleki senses what Joseph
Smith would teach centuries later: "whatsoever you do
not record on earth shall not be recorded in heaven"
(D&C 128:8). As if bursting suddenly out of him, he
forlornly seems to say, "I have a brother. Do you know
where he is?" In the final, minimal space left on these
plates that already have lasted hundreds of years, he
wants to at least mention his missing brother. These
are records destined for fraternal finding and redemption; he should at least try.

Isn't this self-emptying again? Turning the spotlight
away from his own testimony toward this relationship
that keeps him up at night? With this ending, Amaleki
expands his invitation—not just to come to Christ but
to take on others' welfare as our own. Heaven isn't just
about getting in. It isn't simply about eternal domesticity. This is the invitation of the itty bitty books and
the whole Book of Mormon: you are your brother and
sister's keeper. Reading the book gives you access to the
covenant. As God instructs Enos, go to—gather the rest
of the world as well.

Further Reading

Bowen, Matthew L. "'And There Wrestled a Man with Him' (Genesis 32:24): Enos's Adaptations of the Onomastic Wordplay of Genesis." *Interpreter: A Journal of Latter-Day Saint Faith and Scholarship* (Orem, UT) 10 (2014): 151–60. https://journal.interpreterfoundation.org/and-there-wrestled-aman-with-him-genesis-3224-enoss-adaptations-of-theonomastic-wordplay-of-genesis/.

———. "'I Kneeled Down Before My Maker': Allusions to Esau in the Book of Enos." *Interpreter: A Journal of Latter-Day Saint Faith and Scholarship* (Orem, UT) 27 (2017): 29–56. https://journal.interpreterfoundation.org/i-kneeled-down-before-my-maker-allusions-to-esau-in-the-book-of-enos/.

Bushman, Claudia L. "Big Lessons from Little Books." In *2 Nephi 4–Words of Mormon.* The Reader's Book of Mormon 2, edited by Robert A. Rees and Eugene England, vii–xxii. Salt Lake City UT: Signature Books, 2008.

Gardner, Brant A. *Enos through Mosiah.* Second Witness: Analytical and Contextual Commentary on the Book of Mormon 3. Salt Lake City, UT: Greg Kofford Books, 2007.

Hardy, Grant. *Understanding the Book of Mormon: A Reader's Guide.* New York: Oxford University Press, 2010.

Miller, Adam S. *An Early Resurrection: Life in Christ Before You Die.* Provo, UT: Neal A. Maxwell Institute for Religious Scholarship, 2018.

Seely, David R. "Enos and the Words Concerning Eternal Life." In *The Book of Mormon: Jacob through Words of*

Mormon, To Learn with Joy: Papers from the Fourth Annual Book of Mormon Symposium, 1988, edited by Monte S. Nyman and Charles D. Tate, Jr. 235–50. Book of Mormon Symposium Series 4. Provo, UT: Religious Studies Center, Brigham Young University, 1990.

Smith, Julie M. "BMGD #14: Enos, Jarom, Omni, Words of Mormon." *Times and Seasons* (blog), 2 April 2012. https://www.timesandseasons.org/harchive/2012/04/bmgd-14-enos-jarom-omni-words-of-mormon/.

Sperry, Sidney B. *Omni and the Words of Mormon.* Provo, UT: Foundation for Ancient Research and Mormon Studies (FARMS), 1980.

Tanner, John S. "Literary Reflections on Jacob and His Descendants." In *The Book of Mormon: Jacob through Words of Mormon, To Learn with Joy: Papers from the Fourth Annual Book of Mormon Symposium, 1988,* edited by Monte S. Nyman and Charles D. Tate, Jr. 251–70. Book of Mormon Symposium Series 4. Provo, UT: Religious Studies Center, Brigham Young University, 1990.

Welch, John W. "The Father's Command to Keep Records in the Small Plates of Nephi." Preliminary report, FARMS, Provo, UT, September 1984.

Whiting, Gary R. "The Testimony of Amaleki." In *The Book of Mormon: Jacob through Words of Mormon, To Learn with Joy: Papers from the Fourth Annual Book of Mormon Symposium, 1988,* edited by Monte S. Nyman and Charles D. Tate, Jr., 295–306. Book of Mormon Symposium Series 4. Provo, UT: Religious Studies Center, Brigham Young University, 1990.

Endnotes

SERIES INTRODUCTION

1. Elder Neal A. Maxwell, "The Children of Christ," university devotional, Brigham Young University, Provo, UT, 4 February 1990, https://speeches.byu.edu/talks/neal-a-maxwell_children-christ/.

2. Elder Neal A. Maxwell, "The Inexhaustible Gospel," university devotional, Brigham Young University, Provo, UT, 18 August 1992, https://speeches.byu.edu/talks/neal-a-maxwell/inexhaustible-gospel/.

3. Elder Neal A. Maxwell, "The Book of Mormon: A Great Answer to 'The Great Question,'" address, Book of Mormon Symposium, Brigham Young University, Provo, UT, 10 October 1986, reprinted in *The Voice of My Servants: Apostolic Messages on Teaching, Learning, and Scripture,* ed. Scott C. Esplin and Richard Neitzel Holzapfel (Provo, UT: Religious Studies Center, Brigham Young University; Salt Lake City: Deseret Book, 2010), 221–38, https://rsc.byu.edu/archived/voice-my-servants/book-mormon-great-answer-great-question.

INTRODUCTION

1. I am grateful to Spencer Fluhman and the Maxwell Institute for the opportunity to write about the itty bitty books. Lance Larsen and other colleagues in the BYU English department offered much-appreciated support. Many have helped the writing process. The Maxwell Institute editorial team, Lisa and Will Allred, Lisette Allred, Emily Brown, Carter Charles, Michele Coleman, Angela and Obi Ezeonyeka, Katy Fernandez, James Goldberg, Kristine Haglund, Reed and Kathy Harris, Erik and Angela Harris, Vaughn and Jenni Harris, Chad and Debbie Harris, Tessa Hauglid, Jenny Hill, Louise and Will Jeter, Ellis Jeter, Peter Leman, Camille Messick, Sam Niven, Julie Pesqueira, Rebecca Roberts, Adam Stokes, Jenny Webb, and Taylore Wintch gave useful feedback and other help. Conversations with Kim Berkey, Mike Berkey, Liz Fenton, Deidre Green, Ashley

Groesbeck, Adrienne Martin and Loren Thomas, Adam Miller, Ben and Christy Spackman, Shauna Summers, Ruth and Doug Thomas, and Rosalynde Welch strengthened me and the ideas here. I express special gratitude to Joe and Karen Spencer whose feedback made every part of this volume better, and who show me the sweetness of friendship through the Book of Mormon. I have spent more of my young son's life working on this project than not; watching both book and boy grow recommits me to the covenant. Finally, more thanks than I can say go to Edje Jeter who has blessed this undertaking since our first phone call about it. His help is on every page, and it would have been impossible without him. I'm so glad we get to do this together.

2. It's pretty clear that the lost pages included the beginning of the Book of Mosiah because unlike the other books Mormon abridges, Mosiah dives right in without a summarizing preface. See Don Bradley, *The Lost 116 Pages: Reconstructing the Book of Mormon's Missing Stories* (Salt Lake City, UT: Greg Kofford Books, 2019) for more details about what was in Lehi's record.

3. Joseph M. Spencer, *1st Nephi: a brief theological introduction* (Provo, UT: Neal A. Maxwell Institute for Religious Scholarship, 2020), see chapters 1 and 2.

4. Terryl Givens, *2nd Nephi: a brief theological introduction* (Provo, UT: Neal A. Maxwell Institute for Religious Scholarship, 2020), 6; see also Part I.

5. See Deidre Nicole Green, *Jacob: a brief theological introduction* (Provo, UT: Neal A. Maxwell Institute for Religious Scholarship, 2020), 102.

1

1. How do we account for this enormous generational span? Some propose that Enos may not have been Jacob's direct son but, rather, a descendant, given that sometimes the Hebrew word for "son of" (ben) can be used to refer to a later direct descendant as well. But Jacob says, "I said unto my son Enos: Take these plates. And I told him the things which my brother Nephi had commanded me, and he promised obedience unto the commands" (Jacob 7:27). We cannot explain the time span by assuming that Enos and Jacob's lives did not overlap because Jacob describes the handoff. Likewise, Enos recalls the words he had "often heard [his] father speak" (Enos

1:3). He is not drawing on his father's words from the writing alone. The size of the apparent generation gap between Jacob and Enos is unusual and even unlikely, but without a more probable explanation, in this commentary I assume that Jacob is Enos's father.

2. Jacob tells that Nephi "anointed a man to be a king and a ruler over his people" but does not specify that this man was related to Nephi (Jacob 1:9).

3. This passage is just one of several that highlight how Lamanite society gives greater relative value and priority to women than the Nephites do. Deidre Green discusses this in her volume in this series. See especially chapter 4 in *Jacob: a brief theological introduction*. Joseph M. Spencer and Kimberly Matheson Berkey propose that this difference between the Lamanites and Nephites may account for the Nephites' destruction and the Lamanites' survival. See their essay, "'Great Cause to Mourn': The Complexity of *The Book of Mormon*'s Presentation of Gender and Race," in *Americanist Approaches to* The Book of Mormon, ed. Elizabeth Fenton and Jared Hickman (Oxford: Oxford University Press, 2019), 298–320.

4. The three instances are Enos 1:10, D&C 84:59, and Zechariah 2:12.

5. Deidre Green offers a related insight about the need for the "wild" branches in her volume in this series. See her reading of the olive tree allegory in *Jacob: a brief theological introduction*, chapter 5.

6. "Letter to William W. Phelps, 22 July 1840," Joseph Smith Letterbook 2, p. 158, *The Joseph Smith Papers*, https://www.josephsmithpapers. org/paper-summary/letter-to-william-w-phelps-22-july-1840/2.

7. The Church of Jesus Christ of Latter-day Saints (website). Elizabeth Maki, "A People Prepared: West African Pioneer Preached the Gospel before Missionaries," *Pioneers in Every Land*. https://history.churchof jesuschrist.org/article/ghana-pioneer-jwb-johnson?lang=eng.

8. Paul Kagame, interview with Humans of New York, 25 October 2018. Kagame also said: "It might not seem possible for a nation to heal from genocide so quickly. And some might think that our reconciliation is surface level. But it runs deeper than that. If we were truly a nation playing 'make believe,' our progress would have been impossible. Rwanda's per capita GDP has grown nearly 500% since the genocide. And I understand that economics might seem like a dry subject, but you must consider what it represents. It represents Rwandans working together. And trading together. And trusting each other. It represents a consensus that our best future is a shared one. Without true reconciliation, we'd have never come this far. Do tribes still exist in Rwanda? Of course. There will always

be divisions between us. I can't ask people to forget about these things. But I tell them: 'Consider the ways that we are a single tribe. We all speak one language. We all have the same culture, and dances, and behaviors. So be proud of who you are. But also be proud of being Rwandan. Because that is something all of us are." https://www.humansofnewyork.com/post/179444155511/it-might-not-seem-possible-for-a-nation-to-heal.

9. W. H. Auden, "September 1, 1939," in *Another Time* (London: Faber and Faber, 1940), 112–15. Note that the poem appeared earlier under a slightly different title ("September: 1939," in *New Republic* 100, no. 1298 [18 October 1939]: 297) and that Auden removed or changed the quoted line in some subsequent publications.

10. Neal A. Maxwell, "Consecrate Thy Performance," April 2002 general conference of The Church of Jesus Christ of Latter-day Saints, https://www.churchofjesuschrist.org/study/general-conference/2002/04/consecrate-thy-performance?lang=eng.

11. For representative examples, see Jarom 1:3, 7; Alma 44:18; and Mormon 4:18.

12. The preceding ideas and quotations in this paragraph are all from Spencer, *1st Nephi: a brief theological introduction*, chapter 4. See pages 78 and 76 for quotations.

2

1. Laman and Lemuel's immediate response in 1 Nephi 16:1 suggests that they felt Nephi had been personal and pointed in his explanation about filthiness.

2. Royal Skousen argues that "rejected" in 1 Nephi 15:36 was "separated" in the earliest text. Either way, there was an incipient association of Lamanites with filthiness. Skousen, ed., "1 Nephi 15:36," in *Analysis of Textual Variants of the Book of Mormon, Part 1,* Critical Text of the Book of Mormon 4 (Provo, UT: Foundation for Ancient Research and Mormon Studies [FARMS], 2014), 334; also available at https://interpreterfoundation.org/books/atv/p1/.

3. See Green, *Jacob: a brief theological introduction*, chapter 4.

4. I learned of this interpretation in conversation with Joseph Spencer and by attending one of his classroom lectures.

5. Here again Jacob discusses the Lamanites' cursing. I read this as Jacob saying that the Nephites are "filthier" than the Lamanites in spite of the Lamanites' cursing. This indicates Jacob's own investment in these racist conventions, but it still illustrates the idea that filthiness is associated with Nephite prejudice toward the Lamanites.

6. See Brant A. Gardner, *Enos through Mosiah,* Second Witness: Analytical and Contextual Commentary on the Book of Mormon 3 (Salt Lake City, UT: Greg Kofford Books, 2008), 29–30, for his discussion of Meso-american religious practices and of Deuteronomy 12:15–16.

7. See Kimberly Matheson Berkey, *Helaman: a brief theological introduction* (Provo, UT: Neal A. Maxwell Institute for Religious Scholarship, 2020), also in this series, for an extended meditation on what we may not know or notice.

8. See Adam Miller's introduction to Mormon in this series. Miller describes Mormon's book as "a beginner's guide to the end of the world." Adam S. Miller, *Mormon: a brief theological introduction* (Provo, UT: Neal A. Maxwell Institute for Religious Scholarship, 2020), chapter 1.

9. See John S. Tanner, "Literary Reflections on Jacob and His Descendants," in *The Book of Mormon: Jacob through Words of Mormon*, *To Learn with Joy: Papers from the Fourth Annual Book of Mormon Symposium, 1988,* ed. Monte S. Nyman and Charles D. Tate, Jr., Book of Mormon Symposium Series 4, 251–70 (Provo, UT: Religious Studies Center, Brigham Young University, 1990).

10. What we now know as sections 137 and 138 were approved to be added to the Pearl of Great Price in 1976. In 1979 it was announced that they would be moved to the Doctrine and Covenants starting with the 1981 edition of the scriptures. They were received, though, in 1836 and 1918, respectively.

11. See D. Todd Christofferson, "Preparing for the Lord's Return," April 2019 general conference of The Church of Jesus Christ of Latter-day Saints, https://www.churchofjesuschrist.org/study/general-conference/2019/04/44christofferson?lang=eng.

3

1. In dictation order, the Words of Mormon follow the book of Omni, but they are not labeled as a "book."

2. Gardner, *Enos through Mosiah,* 38–39.

3. *The Book of Mormon: Another Testament of Jesus Christ*, ed. Grant Hardy, Maxwell Institute Study Edition, (Provo, UT: Neal A. Maxwell Institute for Religious Scholarship, 2018), Omni 1:6nD.

4. 3 Nephi 11:29 also uses the word "contention" in this way. See Joseph M. Spencer, *An Other Testament: On Typology*, 2nd ed. (Provo, UT: Neal A. Maxwell Institute for Religious Scholarship, 2016), 107–109, for a discussion of how the Nephites were divided on the question of the proper way to baptize.

5. Alma talks about the Liahona in this exchange with Helaman; however, the narrative does not explicitly point to it as with the other artifacts handed down. But Joseph Smith records seeing the Liahona with the records when he found Mormon's compilation at the Hill Cumorah. Because it was preserved to that late date, presumably, the Liahona would have been part of the collection that was conferred from one generation to the next.

6. Lehi prophesied that the brass plates would go forth to every nation, kindred, tongue, and people, and specifically to the descendants of Lehi and Sariah (see 1 Ne. 5:17–18).

7. See, for example, John L. Sorenson, "The 'Brass Plates' and Biblical Scholarship" *Dialogue* 10, no. 4 (1977): 31–39, esp. 33–34, 36–37.

8. See my chapter, "Covenant Obligation to Scripture as Covenant Obligation to Family," in *Christ and Antichrist: Reading Jacob 7*, ed. Adam S. Miller and Joseph M. Spencer (Provo, UT: Neal A. Maxwell Institute for Religious Scholarship, 2017), 111–24.

9. I am grateful to Matthew Wickman for this insight.

10. The commenter was Richard Bushman in our ward's gospel doctrine class in the mid-2010s.

Editions of the
Book of Mormon

Most Latter-day Saints are familiar principally with the official edition of the Book of Mormon published in 2013 by The Church of Jesus Christ of Latter-day Saints. It contains the canonical text of the book, divided into chapters of relatively even length with numbered verses for ease of access. Its footnotes aim to assist readers in seeking doctrinal understanding.

Other Book of Mormon editions are available and often helpful. Among these are official editions from earlier in the scripture's publishing history, which are relatively accessible. There are also editions published recently by a variety of presses meant to make the text more readable. Both types of editions are referred to throughout *Book of Mormon: brief theological introductions*. Also of importance (and occasionally referred to) are the manuscript sources for the printed editions of the Book of Mormon.

manuscript sources

Unfortunately, the original manuscript of the Book of Mormon was damaged during the nineteenth century, but substantial portions of it remain. All known extant portions have been published in typescript in Royal Skousen, ed., *The Original Manuscript of the Book of Mormon: Typographical Facsimile of the Extant Text* (Provo, UT: Foundation for Ancient Research and Mormon Studies [FARMS], 2001). A future volume of the Joseph Smith Papers will publish images of the extant manuscript, along with a typescript.

After completing the original manuscript's dictation, Joseph Smith assigned Oliver Cowdery to produce a second manuscript copy of the text. That manuscript has been called the printer's manuscript since it was designed for use by the first printer of the Book of Mormon. The printer's manuscript, which is more or less entirely intact, also contains corrections and other editorial markings inserted when the second (1837) edition of the Book of Mormon was being prepared. A typescript of the printer's manuscript can be found in Royal Skousen, ed., *The Printer's Manuscript of the Book of Mormon: Typographical Facsimile of the Entire Text in Two Parts,*

2 vols. (Provo, UT: FARMS, 2001). Full color images of the manuscript were subsequently published along with a transcript in the Joseph Smith Papers: Royal Skousen and Robin Scott Jensen, eds., *Printer's Manuscript of the Book of Mormon*, 2 parts, Revelations and Translations 3 (Salt Lake City, UT: Church Historian's Press, 2015). The images and transcript of the printer's manuscript are also available at the Joseph Smith Papers website (www.josephsmithpapers. org/the-papers/revelations-and-translations/jsppr3).

historical editions

Multiple editions of the Book of Mormon were published during the lifetime of Joseph Smith. The first edition, published in Palmyra, New York, in 1830, appeared without versification and with fewer chapter divisions than the present canonical text. The text of the 1830 edition is available electronically at the Joseph Smith Papers website (www.josephsmithpapers.org/the-papers/revelations-and-translations/jsppr4) and in print through various publishers as a replica edition. The 1830 text is also available in Robert A. Rees and Eugene England, eds., *The Reader's Book of Mormon* (Salt Lake City, UT: Signature Books, 2008), which is divided into seven pocket-sized volumes (each with an introduction by a scholar).

Joseph Smith introduced numerous minor changes into the text of the Book of Mormon when it was prepared for a second edition in 1837. Many of these changes are marked in the printer's manuscript. Most were aimed at correcting grammatical issues, but some, in a small handful of cases, were also aimed at clarifying the meaning of the text or its doctrinal implications. The 1837 edition is available electronically at the Joseph Smith Papers website (www. josephsmithpapers.org/the-papers/revelations-and-translations/jsppr4).

A third edition was prepared under Joseph Smith's direction in 1840, and evidence makes clear that the original manuscript was consulted carefully in preparing this edition. Some important errors in the earlier editions were corrected, further grammatical improvements were introduced, and a few other changes were made to the text for purposes of clarification. The 1840 edition can be read at the Joseph Smith Papers website (www.josephsmithpapers.org /the-papers/revelations-and-translations/jsppr4). It forms the basis for at least one printed edition as well: *The Book of Mormon*, trans. Joseph Smith Jr. (New York: Penguin Books, 2008), which contains a helpful introduction by Laurie Maffly-Kipp, a scholar of American religious history.

One other edition of the Book of Mormon appeared during the lifetime of Joseph Smith—an 1841 British edition, which was largely based on the 1837 edition and therefore lacked corrections and other improvements that appear in the 1840 edition. It, too, is available electronically at the Joseph Smith Papers website (www.josephsmithpapers.org/the-papers/revelations-and-translations/jsppr4).

In 1879, Latter-day Saint apostle Orson Pratt completed one of the more influential editions of the Book of Mormon published after Joseph Smith's death. Pratt lamented that too many Latter-day Saints left the scripture unread on the shelf. He sought to create an easier reading experience by dividing up the originally long chapters and adding verse numbers—revisions which have largely remained unchanged in the Church's official edition to the present. He also pioneered a system of cross-references and other explanatory footnotes. Most of Pratt's notes were removed or replaced in subsequent official editions—most thoroughly in the Church's 1981 edition when new descriptive chapter headings were introduced. These headings can still be found, with a few minor updates, in the 2013 edition.

A detailed and helpful devotional treatment of the publication history of the Book of Mormon can be found in Richard E. Turley Jr. and William W. Slaughter, *How We Got the Book of Mormon* (Salt Lake City, UT: Deseret Book, 2011). These authors trace developments in the format and study apparatuses used to present the text of the Book of Mormon to audiences from the 1850s to the present.

study and reading editions

The most important scholarly editions of the Book of Mormon are Grant Hardy, ed., *The Book of Mormon: A Reader's Edition* (Urbana and Chicago: University of Illinois Press, 2003); and Royal Skousen, ed., *The Book of Mormon: The Earliest Text* (New Haven, CT: Yale University Press, 2009).

Hardy's edition repackages the text of the 1921 public domain edition of the Book of Mormon. It contains a helpful introduction, a series of useful appendices, and a straightforward presentation of the text in a highly readable format. Footnotes are minimal—they are used only to clarify direct references or allusions within the text, to track dates, or to alert readers about original chapter divisions. This edition contains modern chapter and verse divisions, but they are unobtrusively typeset. The text is presented in straightforward paragraphs, with one-line headings marking text divisions. Poetry is set off in poetic lines, as in modern editions of the Bible.

Skousen's edition is the result of his quarter-century-long work with the manuscript and printed sources for the Book of Mormon text. The edition aims to reproduce as closely as can be reconstructed the words originally dictated by Joseph Smith to his scribes. Chapter and verse divisions familiar from recent editions are in the text (and symbols mark original chapter breaks), but the text is presented in what Skousen calls "sense lines"—each line containing (on Skousen's reconstruction) approximately what the prophet would have dictated at one time before pausing to allow his scribe to write. The edition contains helpful introductory material and a summary appendix noting significant differences between *The Earliest Text* and the current official edition. It is otherwise without any apparatus for the reader.

The most significant edition of the Book of Mormon deliberately constructed for a lay reading audience is Grant Hardy, ed., *The Book of Mormon: Another Testament of Jesus Christ,* Maxwell Institute Study Edition (Salt Lake City and Provo, UT: Neal A. Maxwell Institute for Religious Scholarship, Deseret Book, and BYU Religious Studies Center, 2018). In this edition, Hardy uses the text of the 2013 official edition of the Book of Mormon but presents it in a readable way for everyday students of the volume. This edition reproduces the best of what appears in Hardy's *Reader's Edition* but adds further resources in the introductory and appendix materials. The footnotes are updated and expanded to include variant readings from the original and printer's manuscripts, and to provide notes about other textual details. The body of the text is presented, as in the *Reader's Edition*, in a straightforward fashion, readable and interrupted only by one-line headings. Modern chapter and verse divisions, as well as original chapter divisions, are easily visible.

Index

124

Colophon

The text of the book is typeset in Arnhem,
Fred Smeijer's 21st-century-take on late
18th-century Enlightenment-era letterforms
known for their sturdy legibility and clarity
of form. Captions and figures are typset in
Quaadraat Sans, also by Fred Smeijers.
The book title and chapter titles are typeset
in Thema by Nikola Djurek.

Printed on Domtar Lynx 74 gsm,
Forest Stewardship Council (FSC) Certified.

Printed by Brigham Young University Print & Mail Services

Woodcut illuminations **Brian Kershisnik**
Book design & typography **Douglas Thomas**
Charts **Douglas Thomas, Sage Perez**
Production typesetting **Natalie Miles, Ruth Eldredge Thomas**

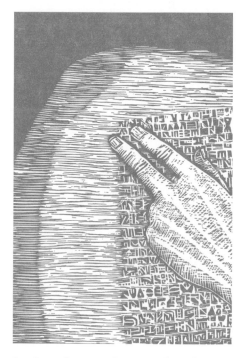

Omni 1:20 there was a large stone brought unto him with engravings on it; and he did interpret the engravings by the gift and power of God.